Osprey Modelling • 34

Modelling the P-51 Mustang

Stan Spooner

Consultant editor Robert Oehler • Series editors Marcus Cowper and Nikolai Bogdanovic

First published in 2007 by Osprey Publishing
Midland House, West Way, Botley, Oxford OX2 0PH, UK
443 Park Avenue South, New York, NY 10016, USA
E-mail: info@ospreypublishing.com

ISBN 978 1 84176 941 7

Editorial by Ilios Publishing Ltd, Oxford, UK (www.iliospublishing.com)
Page layout by Servis Filmsetting Ltd, Manchester, UK
Typeset in Monotype GillSans and ITC Stone Serif
Index by Alan Thatcher
Originated by United Graphics Pte Ltd, Singapore
Printed and bound in China through Bookbuilders

07 08 09 10 11   10 9 8 7 6 5 4 3 2 1

A CIP catalogue record for this book is available from the British Library.

FOR A CATALOGUE OF ALL BOOKS PUBLISHED BY OSPREY MILITARY
AND AVIATION PLEASE CONTACT:

NORTH AMERICA
Osprey Direct, c/o Random House Distribution Center, 400 Hahn Road,
Westminster, MD 21157, USA
E-mail: info@ospreydirect.com

ALL OTHER REGIONS
Osprey Direct UK, P.O. Box 140 Wellingborough, Northants, NN8 2FA, UK
E-mail: info@ospreydirect.co.uk

www.ospreypublishing.com

Photographic credits

All photographs appearing in this book were taken by the authors, Stan Spooner, Brian Criner, Mark Glidden and Marcus Nicholls.

Acknowledgements

This has been a long process. Not only the creation of this book but getting to this point in the hobby. From sitting at the kitchen table at the age of six with my father, Mel, as we built my first model together, to my dear friend Bob Richards reintroducing m to not only the hobby but also the art of modeling. For me, to get to this point in the hobby, it has taken a lot of patience from family and I must say my thanks. First, let me thank my editor, Marcus Cowper, for his infinite patience and support during this endeavour. Next and most importantly, I must thank my family, in particular my amazing and beautiful wife, Gerri, who has been kind enough to put up with me through this entire process and my daughters, Lauren and Kylee, who have been so kind to a father that has been pretty much MIA while writing this book. I also want to thank my brother, Larry, and my nephew, Robert, for reminding me how fun this hobby can be when you just do it for fun.

As far as friends go, I have the best. It is these friends that have been so helpful during the creation of this book. First, let me thank Bob Oehler for all of his efforts and kind words on my behalf. Next, without these three guys and their talents, this book would not have been possible. Brian Criner, Mark Glidden and Marcus Nicholls were kind enough to lend their amazing talents to this effort and let me say that the book is much better because of there work! Other friends that have helped in many ways whether it was through providing advice, encouragement, helping to find parts and information or just insight and encouragement are Karl Madcharo, Mike Laxton, Dan Clover, Tosh Komine, Charlie Pritchett, Kevin Kuster, Dennis Gerber, Steve Munroe, Mike Armstrong, Valerie Langton, John Quint, Henry Tremblay, Mark Hillier, Fred Medel, Stan Pearce (good catch!), François Verlinden, Lloyd Jones, Mark Jones, as well as Ed Roberts and everyone at the National Air Force Museum.

Lastly and ultimately, I thank the Lord for bringing all of these wonderful people into my life.

Contents

Introduction

Whether or not you agree that the North American P-51 Mustang was the best fighter of World War II, the fact remains that up until its entry into the war, there wasn't a fighter that could carry out the long-range escort mission so vital to the success of the Americans' daylight bombing efforts. Without the escorting of those bombers, US losses would have been much higher and the war much longer and bloodier. Very few aircraft can have such a significant place in history as the P-51 but such is the legacy of this Merlin-powered aircraft.

When the modelling community first had a chance to build the P-51 Mustang in 1/48 scale it was thanks to Hawk over 40 years ago, but as far as creating a true modeller's model, thanks go to Monogram. Over 30 years ago they were the first to issue both the P-51B and the P-51D in this now-popular scale. For the time, they were state of the art with finely moulded details in both the cockpit and wheel wells, raised but delicate panel lines and accurate shape and proportions. With a little bit of work, these kits could be turned into quite a nice model. These kits were all we had until the 1970s when Otaki released their P-51D. This offering was the first to have recessed panel lines, although the detail was somewhat simplified. In the 1980s Hasegawa ushered in the era of modern kit making for this subject with their P-51D. With finely engraved details and modern moulds, this kit was everything the modelling community was looking for. Over the years, the Hasegawa kit has been issued many times with all types of extra parts to make everything from the F-51D to the P-51 used for test purposes with wingtip-mounted jets! In the mid-1990s, Accurate Miniatures decided to pay homage to the unsung Mustangs with Allison engines. Their offerings of these airplanes were Accurate Miniatures' first 1/48-scale kits and by today's standards they look a bit simple; however, they are easily built into beautiful models. The Tamiya P-51D came to the market with superior engineering although a somewhat simplified cockpit. Next came their P-51B, which has a much-improved cockpit and is a truly beautiful kit. Another manufacturer that has come to the market is Classic Airframes with their P-51H, which has an accurate shape and nice resin details. Finally, Modelcraft of Canada has brought us the ultimate incarnation of this family tree, the F-82 Twin Mustang. Whichever variant of this plane you want to build, there is a 1/48-scale kit out there for you.

Building a well-worn P-51A

Subject:	*P-51A*
Primary modeller:	*Mark Glidden*
Paint and final assembly:	*Marcus Nicholls*
Skill level:	*Advanced*
Base kit:	*Accurate Miniatures P-51A Mustang (3402)*
Scale:	*1/48*
Additional detail sets used:	*True Details interior detail set (48481); Ultracast prop blades (48138); Eduard photo-etch detail set (48134); Verlinden exposed Allison engine detail set; Cutting Edge Mk 8 resin gunsight (48156)*
Decals:	*From ICM Models P-51A kit and spares box; Mike Grant 1/48-scale instrument decals*
Paint:	*Various Tamiya acrylics, Hannants' Xtracrylics matte varnish*

Accurate Miniatures' 1/48-scale P-51A in the box

Although a little on the old side, this kit still manages to hold its own against newer offerings. Accurate Miniatures has done a very nice job of moulding the fuselage with separate cowling parts to accommodate the modelling of different versions of the early Mustang.

The cockpit

The two round alignment pins on the inside of the fuselage had to be removed to fit the resin parts. The resin cockpit sidewalls were sanded on a flat piece of sandpaper to remove the backing. This also opened up the spaces between ribs. On the left side of the cockpit, two photo-etch dials from the Eduard set were added, along with styrene disc for the centre of the trim wheel. Using the True Details' resin cockpit set actually requires you to use a combination of resin and kit parts to assemble the cockpit. The Eduard photo-etch rudder pedals were used instead of the resin ones, which were removed. Resin parts were primed with Mr Surfacer 1000, which prepared the parts for painting and helped smooth out the surface. The instrument panel was painted Tamiya XF-1 Black in the recessed area and XF-69 NATO Black on the outside. This was done to give it some depth and interest. A mix of Tamiya XF-3 Yellow (two parts) to XF-5 Green (one part) was used for the interior green. The cockpit was pre-shaded with XF-69 NATO Black. Mike Grant 1/48-scale instrument decals were used on the instrument panel. The dial faces were punched out with a Waldron punch and die. Care must be taken when using these decals, as they scratch easily. Micro-Sol was then applied to get the decals to conform to shape. The flare gun mount was made from .04in. styrene rod, sheet styrene and .5mm springs. A hole was drilled into the side of the fuselage and the rod. The sheet styrene was cut into squares and sanded to the correct shape using a round file. Everything was then carefully glued together. The flare gun mounting hole was then drilled out with a .033in. drill bit. The resin canopy hinges were sanded down and replaced with some spare photo-etch parts.

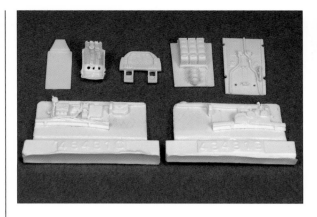

This shows the resin parts that come in the True Details update set. This set adds a great deal of depth and detail to the simple kit interior.

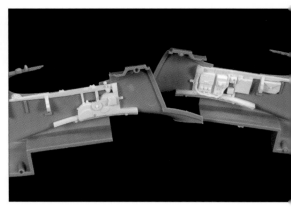

This shows how the parts fit into the cockpit walls.

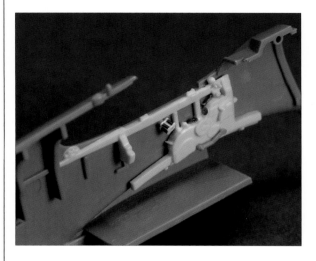

This view shows the scratch-built flare gun port. The port was made from Evergreen stock and small springs picked up at a shop in Japan. This is a key detail that was otherwise missing.

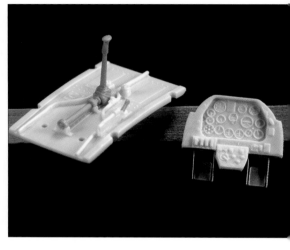

Here is the resin cockpit floor and instrument panel using kit stick and photo-etch pedals.

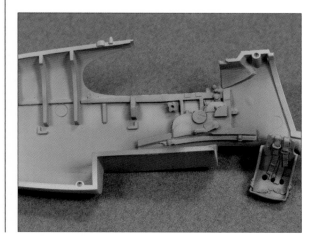

Here, the cockpit has been painted with a basecoat of interior green and then highlighted.

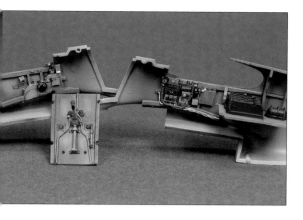

This shot shows the completed cockpit before assembly. All details have been brush painted with acrylic paint.

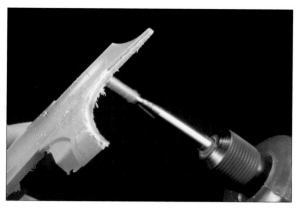

Plastic was ground away from the fuselage wall with a Dremel to mount the Verlinden exposed engine.

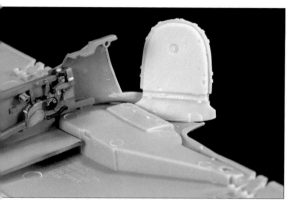

The back of the resin firewall fits easily into the newly cut fuselage walls.

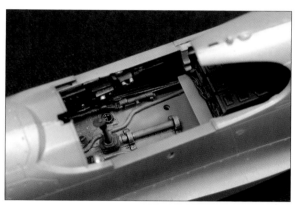

After the fuselage has been assembled, the cockpit interior shows a great deal of detail and depth.

The cockpit was post-shaded with Tamiya XF-4 Yellow Green. The wooden map case was painted with a base coat of Tamiya Buff BF-57, which was then covered with a thin mix of burnt sienna, burnt umber and raw sienna oil paints. Once it had been given a few minutes to dry, light strokes with a brush were applied to simulate the wood grain. Various size discs were punched from sheet styrene and placed on the sidewalls as additional detail was needed. A firing button was also added. Eduard photo-etch placards were used throughout the cockpit and these added a great deal of detail otherwise difficult to achieve. The interior was drybrushed with a mix of sap green, titanium white and indian yellow oil paints while the instrument dial faces were given a drop of Future floor wax to simulate the glass lenses. The resin cockpit floor was too narrow by ³⁄₂in. so a piece of strip styrene was glued into place and sanded to shape to fill the gap. The cockpit was sprayed with Future to prepare it for an oil paint wash. It also served to help seal in the photo-etch placards. A silver pencil was used to add some wear to the cockpit interior. MIG Productions' Euro Dust pigment was mixed with Tamiya thinner and spread around the cockpit floor for a mud/dirt effect. Once it had dried, the excess was removed with a paintbrush. Next .0075in. wire was used to make rudder cables, which were attached to the extensions on the rudder pedals. The instrument panel with the rudder cable wires attached was inserted through the front of the fuselage opening, making sure the rudder cable wires were correctly placed. The instrument panel was then glued into place.

A piece of .015in. solder wire was used for the cable running to the ceiling mounted radio box behind the seat. The resin seat armour plate had to be trimmed ⅛in. to get it to fit. Styrene discs were glued to the attachment point on the cockpit sidewalls to give the A-frame rollover bar enough height. The final step for the cockpit was to apply a coat of Testors' Dullcote. The kit gunsight didn't look anything like the N3 gunsight used in the P-51A and so a Cutting Edge Mk 8 resin gunsight was used as the foundation for a new version. The top and side details were removed and a piece of styrene rod was glued to the bottom to form the base. Pieces of styrene rod were glued to each side to form the detail. To make the lens, a piece of clear acetate was cut to the correct shape and glued on with white glue.

Next, the kit canopy was cut into three sections using a micro saw. Spare photo-etch pieces were cut to shape to make the two hinges for the fold-down section of the canopy. The base of the fold-down section was made from .01in. strip styrene. The two ribs on the bottom of the base were made from .01in. square strips. The handle was fabricated from .01in. brass wire.

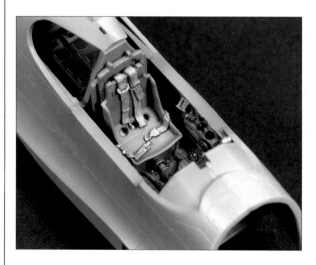

Here you get a good view of the cockpit after the installation of the seat and armour plate.

A scratch-built gunsight was made to better represent the real thing.

Here the newly scratch-built gunsight is mounted on the cowling.

Photo-etch and scratch-built parts have been added to the roof behind the cockpit.

Here you see the scratch-built detail and the photo-etch parts added to the folding canopy.

Building the landing gear

First, I cut the tailwheel strut in order to angle the wheel. I then painted the tailwheel well with Aircraft Colour US Interior Yellow and the strut with Alclad Steel. I then added .0075in. wires to represent the tailwheel door-closing mechanism. The tailwheel strut and door interior was given a wash of charcoal black, burnt sienna and burnt umber oils. I noticed that the landing-gear struts were lacking the openings in the torsion arms so I drilled two holes into each arm, opened them up and shaped them with a hobby knife. I then painted the struts with Tamiya XF-16 Silver while Bare Metal 'Ultra Bright Chrome' foil was used for the strut oleos. I used .02in. insulated wire to represent the brake lines with each end of the wire the insulation was removed to represent tubing. Lastly, I flattened .01in. solder wire and cut it to size to make the hose fasteners.

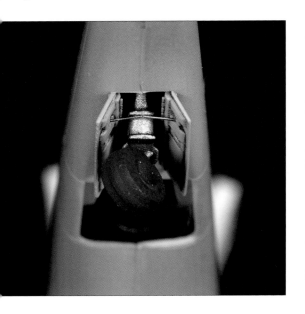

The tailwheel is seen here after it has been detailed, painted and weathered.

Plumbing and other details have been added to the strut using wire, solder and tape.

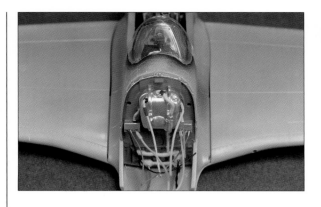

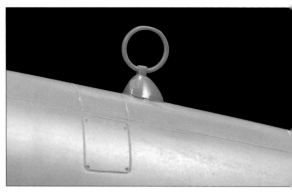

In this shot, you see the gap between fuselage and wing is evident. This is never fun to deal with, but was easily solved with some Evergreen sheet plastic and Zap-A-Gap glue.

The DF loop taken from a Tamiya P-47 kit. It was thinned out and the mounting 'cone' was shaped to fit.

Now to the fuselage

I made a new hot air exit ramp from a sanded-down piece from the Tamiya P-51B kit, as it had a better shape. I also sanded down the front edge of the windscreen with 400-grit sandpaper wrapped around a wooden dowel. I found the radiator scoop piece was too narrow and left a noticeable step on either side when placed up against the fuselage. To fix this, I glued a strip of .020in styrene to the side of the scoop, covered it with Mr Surfacer 500 and sanded it down when dry. To better represent the DF loop, I used one from the Tamiya P-47D kit. This was the perfect size and only needed to be thinned a little.

The Verlinden exposed engine

When planning this build, I felt that it was vital to use the exposed engine designed for this kit by Verlinden. I started by using a Dremel tool to grind down the raised lip along the front edge of the fuselage to make room for the resin firewall, which was then smoothed out with a metal file. The Verlinden instructions tell you to remove 3mm from the inside forward portion of the wheel well to fit the firewall. However, removing 3mm would have you inside the wheel well and I decided to fit it without removing the material. Doing this required a lot of careful test-fitting, and my recommendation is to work slowly and check your progress often. The lower back of the resin firewall had to be

The resin firewall has been primed and pre-shaded.

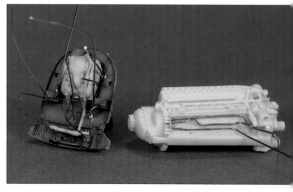

Here you see the firewall and engine after they have been 'wired-up' using solder and copper wire. This will allow the final model to look very busy.

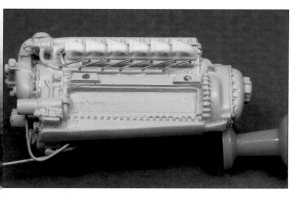

In this shot, you see the resin exhausts have been added to the primed engine.

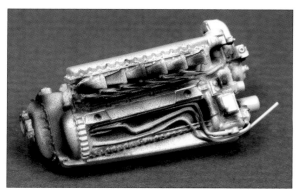

Here you see the engine has been primed and pre-shaded.

sanded down to help the fit. To simulate plumbing and wires in the engine I used varying thicknesses of solder wire, with pieces of Tamiya tape used to form the hose connectors, which were tacked over the wire with cyanoacrylate (CA) glue. The Ultracast exhausts were used, as the detail was somewhat better than the Verlinden set. The back of the exhaust stack had to be sanded to get the unit set at the correct angle on the engine block. The lightening holes on the resin engine mounts needed to be opened up. The little 'L'-shaped cowling attachment brackets located on the top of the engine mounts had to be cut off and lowered by ½in. as they interfered with the placement of the engine exhaust stacks. Spark plug wires were made from .01in. solder and the holes to mount them were carefully drilled into the side of the resin engine with a .011in. drill bit. I brushed Mr Surfacer 500 into areas of the engine block that had a rough surface texture to them and, once dry, I then sprayed several coats of Mr Surfacer 1000 over the top. When it came to painting the firewall, it was covered with Tamiya XF-4 Yellow Green. The engine block was sprayed with Gunze Sangyo H337 Blue-Grey and the engine plumbing and supports were painted with Tamiya XF-4 Yellow Green. Lastly, I basecoated the exhaust stacks with dark grey enamel and then weathered them with pastel powders.

This view shows the completed firewall installed.

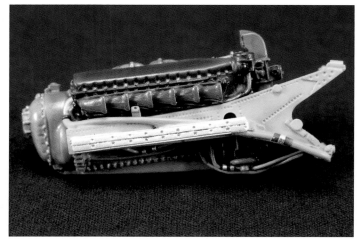

The completed engine and its mounting brackets after painting and ready for installation.

Adding the ordnance

To end up with the best results, I felt it was important to use the bombs from the Tamiya P-47D kit. I coated these with Mr Surfacer 500 and, before it dried, stippled it with a cut-down, stiff paintbrush. This gave the surface of the bomb the textured appearance often found on the actual weapons. To cover a large seam found on the end of each bomb, a circular piece of styrene was punched out and placed on top.

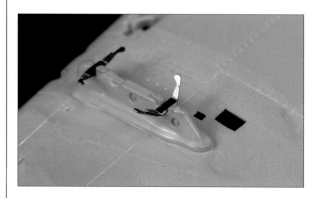

To achieve a greater level of detail, resin and photo-etch bomb racks were added.

To recreate the rough texture found on the actual bombs, thinned Tamiya basic putty has been stippled onto the kit bombs using a blunt brush.

The Verlinden bomb racks were used instead of the kit racks, as they contained a bit more detail. To fill the small gap between the wing and the bomb rack, Mr Surfacer 500 was brushed onto the gap. Once dry, a cotton bud damped with Mr Colour Thinner was wiped over the area to remove the excess filler. I added Eduard photo-etch bomb sway braces and they fitted perfectly into the Verlinden racks.

The wings

The only problem with the wings is that there are large gaps at the wing roots that need to be filled. This was solved by adding some Evergreen sheet stock and CA glue, and by a lot of filling and sanding. The next task was to rescribe the joint line. Lastly, I drilled a .05in. hole into the leading edge of the left wing to create the gun camera opening.

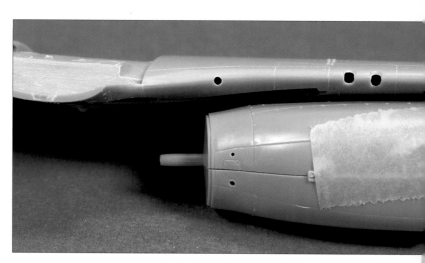

The gun camera and drain holes have been added on the leading edges of the wings and lower cowlings.

The prop

The Ultracast resin propeller was used as it had a thinner, more correct shape. Ultracast supplies only the blades, so the kit hub and spinner have to be used. The kit blades were removed and a .02in. hole was drilled into the hub and into the base of the resin prop blade to accept a brass rod. The rod assures a strong joint. I then glued the resin blades into place and set them at the correct angle.

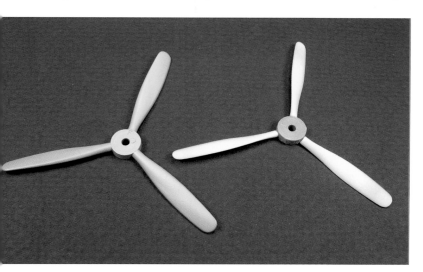

LEFT The thin and elegant shape of the propeller blades was better represented by the Ultracast resin set rather than the kit blades. The old blades are simply cut off of the mounting ring and the new blades were pinned and glued to the ring using brass wire and CA glue.

BELOW One final look at the major assembly before it gets turned over to the 'paint shop'.

Markings

I started off by painting the model with Tamiya XF-62 Olive Drab upper and XF-53 Neutral Grey lower surfaces and then it was time for the markings. The aircraft modelled here is a P-51A of the USAAF 1st ACG (Air Commando Group) based in the huge China/Burma/India (CBI) theatre of operation, during 1943–44. The diagonal white stripe markings were unique to this unit and form an attractive visual device to break up the monotony of the olive drab finish. Due to the relentless demands of combat sorties, little time was available to clean these aircraft, so exhaust staining built up to an extreme degree, with extraordinarily long stains running nearly the full length of the fuselage on both sides. If I had not seen a photograph of this aircraft I would never have created such an extreme weathering effect, so it really does prove just how important it is to gather your references when embarking on a new modelling project.

The decals

Before any weathering was applied, the decals, which were lifted from the ICM P-51A kit, went on, and to facilitate this, an overall coat of Johnson's Klear (Future) was airbrushed onto all surfaces. Daco 'Strong' setting solution was employed to seat the markings properly. Over this, several heavily thinned coats of Hannants' Xtracrylics matt varnish was applied, restoring the near flat lustre required for this project.

Weathering

I used Tamiya's ever-useful XF-57 Buff to begin the exhaust staining process. The paint was thinned heavily (80 per cent thinners to 20 per cent paint), and steadily built up on both sides using an Iwata Custom Micron CM-C Plus airbrush. I lightened the Buff with a few drops of XF-55 Deck Tan and applied a few more strokes over the streaking pattern to add a little more texture.

One notable feature of the exhaust staining on this machine is the vertical rain marks created when it sat unprotected in monsoon conditions. The rain gradually washed off the powdery stains and, to simulate this, I dipped a medium-fine brush in Tamiya acrylic thinner and drew it vertically down the fuselage sides. Absolute precision in this exercise was not required because rain never runs in perfectly straight lines, particularly when running over riveted

The airframe after its coat of straight XF-62 Olive Drab, before the lightened mix was applied. Notice how dark it looks.

A particularly grungy area is at the frontal wing root where it meets the engine cowlings. Brown oil paints were used to create this mucky look.

BELOW The undercarriage bays were painted natural aluminium and given washes of thinned brown oil paints to suggest splashed-up dirt.

BOTTOM A view into the cockpit shows the True Details resin parts. A better than normal view is afforded thanks to the double opening canopy.

heet metal. The white stripes received heavily chipped and frayed edges, articularly on the upper fuselage area where I thought the buffeting might be more intense.

I used a light brown colour mix of oil paint and white (mineral) spirit to ighlight the panel lines on the olive drab painted areas, and a dark brown mix n the lower surfaces; I also used these mixes to create further staining and urface marks to add to the look of a very heavily tarnished airframe. A silver oloured pencil, sharpened to a very fine point, was used to create a matrix of hips and scrapes at the wing roots and engine cowling areas, and MIG 'roductions' Europe Dust pigment was used in small amounts to simulate plashed-up mud around the undercarriage doors and wing undersides.

Here we see the firewall, which carries the Allison oil tank, again cast beautifully by Verlinden Productions in resin. Note the cowling fixing points.

This underside view shows the closed-up main undercarriage doors, a feature of the P-51A variant of the Mustang.

A close-up look at the canopy and firewall. Modellers sometime forget to weather the canopy framing, but these raised strips of aluminium collected a lot of dirt and so are worth taking time over.

Leading edges received quite a lot of paint chips as they are on the front line of airborne debris stirred up by the big three-bladed prop.

With the cowling off, the graceful lines of the Mustang are lost, but the busy engine area makes up for this. Note the red canopy-locking handle.

A good view of that heavy exhaust staining. Effects like this are best built up in thin layers of paint so they can be controlled.

LEFT Weathering a model to this degree is not the norm, but in this case, it is highly accurate.

BELOW This is a great overhead view showing off the Allison V12 engine, nicely cast by Verlinden Productions.

BELOW The spinners of many of the 1st ACG's P-51As were in bare metal, and on the model this was simulated using Alclad II Chrome, toned down with airbrushed-on matt varnish.

BELOW The white bands on the tail also received chips and scrapes. Note the white '18' applied over the code.

British shark – P-51B/Mustang III

Subject:	P-51B/Mustang III
Modeller:	Brian Criner
Skill level:	Advanced
Base kit:	Tamiya North American RAF Mustang III (61047)
Scale:	1/48
Additional detail sets used:	Aires resin gun bay (4241); Ultracast props and spinners (48136); Ultracast flaps/rudder/elevators (48025); Obscuro wheels (48004); Jaguar resin interior (64804); Eduard Color photo-etch placards (FE198); Eduard harness/instrument panel (FE219); Ultracast resin British bombs; Ultracast exhaust stacks (48026)
Decals:	From kit and spares box
Paint:	Testors' Model Master Enamels

An overview

The most obvious problem with Tamiya's P-51B kit is the curved cockpit floor. In addition, the kit sidewalls are pretty basic. A simple and delightful fix to this problem is provided by the Jaguar resin interior. This update provides nicely detailed sidewalls, a seat and a proper floor and radio compartment, including the radiator. To this was added placards and stencils from the Eduard Color photo-etch placard set.

In addition to the cockpit resin, I used aftermarket flaps, exhaust stacks, gear doors, bombs, rudder, elevators, spinner and prop blades provided by Ultracast, making this airplane nearly all resin. The tailwheel doors are photo-etch from Eduard. All of the aftermarket parts were easy replacements, though proper fitting of the armament bays required particularly careful cutting and grinding of the wings to make sure of a good fit. My only complaint about the

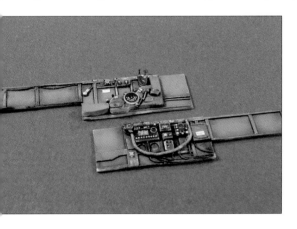

The Jaguar resin sidewalls are an excellent addition to the kit. After painting, weathering and some careful drybrushing, they were enhanced with the addition of placards from the Eduard Color photo-etch placard set.

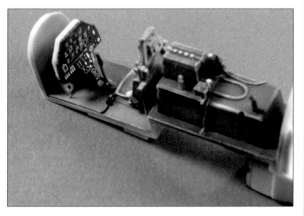

The Jaguar cockpit is more accurate, and much more detailed than the kit-supplied parts. The radiator is moulded into the bottom of the cockpit floor.

Resin components of the cockpit painted and ready for installation. The cockpit sidewalls need to be thinned as much as the resin will allow. The floor component is easily installed, but will still require your total attention when gluing into the fuselage side if you are to avoid annoying alignment and fit problems.

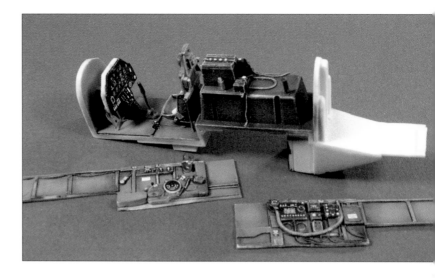

aftermarket armament is that the feed chutes were too short to reach the guns a relatively easy fix with the addition of some cut pieces of sheet styrene.

Gun bays

Before gluing the .50-cal. machine guns into the wing bays, I test-fitted them to see if there were any irregularities of fit in need of attention before they were permanently glued in place. As commonly occurs when using aftermarket kits some areas were problematic. The wing bay holes through which the barrel pass did not line up properly with the leading edge holes. This, of course means either the guns will not be aligned correctly in the bays, or the gun barrels will not be correctly aligned where they protrude from the wing leading edge. In addition, the gun barrels were not long enough to extend out of the wing the proper distance. A simple fix to this problem was to 'dope' over the wing gun ports with red decal tape cut to size. Ground crews in all theatres of action, but particularly in areas where fine sand and dust could foul the guns commonly used this procedure. It was a convenient solution for me because I was not interested in fixing the wing bays and leading edge in order to make the guns line up correctly. In order to make the gun bays a bit more interesting, I added fine solder to the guns to simulate the charging cables. The

The Aires resin gun bays are beautifully moulded and they look fantastic on the finished model. Careful cutting and sanding are necessary in order to achieve a good fit and to get your wing halves closed.

mmo feed chutes connecting the guns to the cast resin trays were a bit rough, nd work was necessary to get the two parts to align correctly. The resin gun ay doors were nicely cast, and were painted and glued into position on various arts of the wings. After gluing the main doors in place, I used a piece of fine teel wire, bent to shape with pliers, to represent the prop bar.

Ultracast propeller, blades and exhaust tacks

he Ultracast prop is a great addition to the kit and much superior to the kit-supplied parts in shape nd overall detail. There are two problems you will ncounter when using this particular aftermarket roduct. In every example I have seen of this offering, he prop blades are warped. I fixed this by simply ending them until I felt they were straight. Second, hen inserting the props, it is important that you use ow-drying glue, as there is no slotting in the spinner o ensure the prop blades are inserted at the proper ngle or blade pitch. I used slow-drying Zap glue, and as able to correct the angle of the blades after serting them into the spinner until I felt their osition looked right. If you are not careful here, you ill end up snapping off a propeller blade.

Ultracast offers some beautiful exhaust stacks, both hrouded and unshrouded, that are simple replacements or the kit parts. The obvious benefit of using these parts is they make the tedious isk of drilling out the individual stacks unnecessary. Originally I used the hrouded exhausts, but when I broke several tubes off while attempting to get he part to seat properly I opted for the unshrouded stacks. In order to create a ealistic, rusted appearance on the stacks I decided to use the Rustall system. The ustall kit involves the use of four different bottles, each of which is to be used in equence to create the a 'rust' effect. One of the bottles contains the 'rusty' igment. Probably out of impatience, I decided to use just this bottle. If you apply beral amounts of this product to a flattened (as opposed to glossy) surface, and low it to dry, it will give a slightly oxidized, rusty look to the finish. I started y painting the stacks with Testors' Burnt Iron mixed with Testors' Titanium. I ollowed this with a liberal coat of Testors' Clear Flat (this gives the Rustall omething to bite into and also protects the paint underneath, which will be amaged by the Rustall if not protected). After applying the Rustall pigment, I lowed several minutes for it to dry, and then applied it again. I continued this ntil I got the proper 'oxidized' look I was after.

This model is carrying quite a bit of resin! In addition to the cockpit and wing guns, aftermarket control surfaces, exhaust, spinner/blades, gear doors and wheels from Ultracast were used.

Painting and decals

nce all of the main fuselage assemblies were completed, the model was prayed with a coat of Mr Surfacer 1000. Once dry, this was buffed with olishing cloth and a buffing wheel in a Dremel tool. Next, the rudder and evators were connected and the model was pre-shaded with Testors' Burnt mber. Pre-shading has fallen out favour with many modellers today, but I still el it is an effective technique for making your model come to life. To prevent he pre-shading from overpowering the finish, I typically use burnt umber ither than black. The trick with pre-shading is to cover it with the topcoat hough to mute it, but not eliminate its effect. My goal is for the pre-shading give tone variation to the finish. Once the top colours were applied, each ction of the finish was post shaded with a slightly lightened version of the ppropriate colour. To prevent a 'whitewash' effect, I usually post-shade with st a drop or two of Testors' Beige or Light Gray (rather than white) added to well-thinned cup of Testors' Clear Flat.

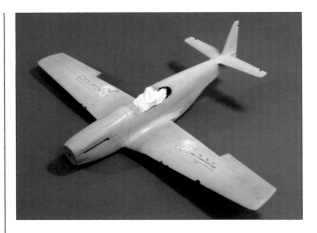

After a careful check of the model to ensure all seams were properly filled, sanded and polished, the entire model was coated with a layer of Mr Surfacer 1000. This incredible product not only acts as a primer, but also fills in minor scratches and defects. Once dry, the surface was thoroughly polished with a buffing wheel chucked in a Dremel.

Once the Mr Surfacer is dry and buffed, the model is pre-shaded using a thin mix of Testors' Model Master Burnt Umber. The pre-shading does not need to be precise, as the pattern will not be easily discernable through the surface paint.

Decals were the kit-supplied offerings. All of the decals went down without incident with the notable exception of the upper wing roundels. For some odd reason, I was unable to get them to set properly and it was necessary to use several applications of Micro-Sol to get them to flatten down. Once all the decals were properly set, I ran a new No. 11 scalpel blade down all the panel lines crossed by the decals and then reapplied the Micro-Sol in the panels to get the decals pulled down into all the lines and dimples.

Next, I painted, assembled and installed the landing gear. In place of the kit wheels I used the very nice offering from Obscuro. To simulate hydraulic line

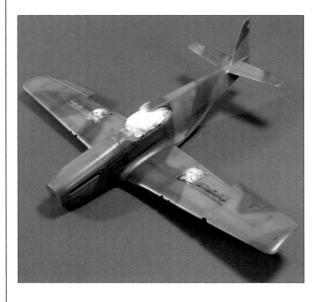

Camouflage paint is applied using Model Master enamels, lightest to darkest. Once the colours have been applied, post-shading is applied using a slightly lightened and well-thinned version of the appropriate surface colour.

Before decaling, the surface was given a coat of Future floor acrylic. This gives the model a smooth surface for the decals to bind to. All of the decals went down with the help of repeated applications of Micro-Sol.

I used solder obtained from Derek Browns' Buffies Best. Once the aircraft is up on its gear, and the gear is properly aligned, it is time to start the weathering process.

Weathering

Weathering begins with a sealing coat of Future floor wax. Since I paint only with enamels, this step is necessary to prevent the solvent in the wash from eating up the paint. It is also necessary to blend the decals into the surface. Once the Future is dry, I coat the entire model with a coat of Testors' Clear Flat. This is a step that most modellers omit or disregard. If a wash is done on the glossy surface created by the Future it is easy to remove the wash pigment and

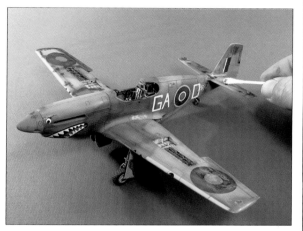

After the decals were set and dry, they were given another coat of Future to blend them into the surface. Once the Future was dry, the model is given one coat of Testors' Clear Flat. This step is necessary before the oil wash so the wash pigment has something to stick to. Next, all panel lines are given a relatively thick wash of Grumbacher Burnt Umber oils.

The wash is wiped out with a cotton bud dipped in Turpenoid. The cleaning process is repeated until the only wash remaining on the model is in the panel lines. This part of the process will undoubtedly wear through the Clear Flat coat and expose some of the gloss protective coat, as is apparent in this picture. Once the wash process is complete, these patchy parts are easily removed by the addition of another, well-thinned, Clear Flat coat.

Using a well-sharpened Prismacolor chrome-coloured pencil, scuff marks and chips were simulated around the wing root area.

Stains from fuel, oil and hydraulic fluid were simulated using a brush dipped into a mix of burnt umber artist oils.

avoid stains, as it doesn't bind very well to the glossy surface. My complaint about this approach is … the wash doesn't bind to the glossy surface! When wiping out a wash applied to a glossy coat, you often end up wiping all of the wash out and therefore defeating the purpose. When a wash is applied to a flat surface the pigment has something to bite into. The problem now faced is the removal of the excess pigment, which has the potential to 'stain' the finish if you are not careful. I have not experienced any real problems with this, and when staining has occurred, it has actually accentuated the weathering rather than detracted from it. My wash is really more of a 'mud' in some areas, than a 'wash'. I actually apply the pigment in a rather thick (but not oily or gummy) consistency to certain areas and in a very watery consistency to others. I wipe the wash out with cotton buds soaked in Turpenoid (a turpentine substitute). Before applying the cotton bud to the surface, I wipe out the excess solvent on an old T-shirt so the cotton bud is moist but not saturated. I continue wiping the surface until I see very little coloration on the cotton bud. If done correctly, the pigment will give a nice highlight to your panel lines that is not as stark as would be the case if you did your wash in black or dark grey. If you inadvertently wipe all of the pigment out of the panel line, it is easy to apply

The exhaust stacks were first painted with Testors' Burnt Iron. After another coat of Clear Flat, the stacks were given a liberal coating of Rustall's rust-coloured pigment. Once dry, the pigment is reapplied and allowed to thoroughly dry again. Repeat the process until you get a look that seems right.

Hydraulic, oil leaks and general grime on the bottom surface of the aircraft is simulated using MIG Productions' pigments placed in various panel lines and then drawn back with a cotton bud and chisel-tip brush.

Stains along the wing were further enhanced by first drawing some Desert Sand MIG pigments back along the wing root. This creates an optimal situation for adding one last wash. The wash is drawn down the panel lines and out into the pigments.

more. The process of wiping out the excess pigment from the wash may wear through your previously applied flat coat, giving the model an odd, 'patchy' appearance with both glossy and flat areas. Not to worry! Add a bit of Testors' Clear Flat to the cup, being sure to keep it well thinned, and spray over the worn areas. The 'glossy' patches will immediately disappear.

Once the main wash is complete, selective other washes are applied, generally to the unusually dirty parts of the plane. Oil and coolant stains on the bottom of the aircraft are well documented in photos. To recreate these stains I used a combination of a thin burnt umber wash, pushed back (from front to back) with air from my airbrush. This takes a bit of practice, as, if you are not careful, it creates a splattered look. The wing roots received repeated, very thin dirty washes. I allowed the wash to get pulled down the panel lines onto the

The resin gun bay covers are crisply cast. The aftermarket kit includes several photo-etch details such as hatch levers.

panels. This gives a nice effect if done on a flat surface and is repeated several times. The wash sticks to the flat surface and gives a realistic stained finish. On top of this staining I used a Prismacolor chrome-coloured pencil to stipple small chips and scuffs in order to represent the wear these high-use areas were prone to.

Bits and pieces

All that was left to do was attach all of the small bits and pieces. After attaching the bombs, flaps, pitot and antennae mast, I attached the painted clear parts. The radio aerial is made from clear nylon thread and was glued to the aircraft using Zap glue and accelerator. The last thing to do was paint all formation lights. Some final weathering was then applied by adding small bits of MIG Productions' pigment powder to the wing roots and the bottom of the aircraft around the radiator. This was then drawn back along the aircraft using a cotton bud and a chisel-tipped brush.

Resin bombs were supplied by Ultracast. Each bomb was pre-shaded and post-shaded. Chipping was done with a Prismacolor pencil as before.

Canopy and glass have been added. The gun bays are ready for finishing.

ABOVE LEFT, ABOVE RIGHT AND LEFT The completed model with all hatches and clear parts in place.

RIGHT A good shot of the bottom of the finished model.

ABOVE LEFT, ABOVE RIGHT AND RIGHT Clear nylon thread was used for the antennae aerial. Steel wire, bent to shape, is used to prop the gun bay doors open.

Creating a 357th FG P-51D

Subject:	P-51D
Modeler:	Stan Spooner
Skill Level:	Intermediate
Base kit:	Tamiya P-51D Mustang 8th AF Ace (61089)
Scale:	1/48
Additional detail sets used:	True Details P-51 seat (48453); Obscuro wheels (48004); Ultracast spinner (48136); Cutting Edge K-14 gunsight (48155); Eduard Color photo-etch placards (FE198); Teknics 105-gal. paper drop tanks
Decals:	From kit and spares box (bits and pieces of an out-of-print AeroMaster sheet)
Paint:	Custom mixes of Tamiya and Gunze acrylic paints

A quick look at Tamiya's 1/48-scale P-51D in the box

As 1/48-scale Mustangs go, it is my opinion this is the best offering available today. Originally released in 1995, there have been several updates and variations released since. For this build, I used the 2003 '8th AF Ace' version.

The cockpit and wheel wells are lacking in detail, and what is provided in these areas is elementary and in some cases misrepresented. As for the surface detail, it is generally good with clear panel lines that will hold up under even a generous amount of paint. The kit comes with both paper and 'tear-drop' type fuel tanks. It also comes with two 500lb bombs for portraying a ground-attack version.

My subject was flown by Tommy Hayes, the commander of the 364th Fighter Squadron. He scored 8.5 aerial victories in total, all in Europe. 'Frenesi', pronounced 'free-and-easy', bears the name of Artie Shaw's hit song from 1939.

Adding some detail and paint to the cockpit

The first thing I added to the cockpit was a new True Details seat. It comes with everything except diagonal seat supports and I added these using .15mm pieces of Evergreen strip. I cleaned up and thinned out the rudder pedals and cut away the plastic returns along the sides of each pedal. Thin copper wire was used to simulate the wiring on the radio, and the same thin wire was wrapped around some brass wire and then bent in shape to simulate the oxygen hose. A small drop of CA glue and I had no slippage problem when the coils were being bent into the hose's final shape. The trim wheel is poorly represented by a tall, vertical piece of plastic with a curved top. To fix the problem, all I did was take off the offending shaft of plastic and replace it with a couple of punched plastic discs. Hose and wire attachment straps were made using Tamiya tape secured in place with a touch of extra thin CA glue. One of the last modifications made to the cockpit was to remove the shaft of plastic coming up from the floorboard on the right side that is supposed to represent the BC-438 control. In all of the reference photos I had, it didn't look like that. It was in fact supposed to be a box with a sloping top mounted to the sidewall with the oxygen hose running underneath. To represent this, I cut it off of the floorboard (after I had already painted it), cut the

This shows the True Details seat used with simple Evergreen support struts in place.

The Tamiya rudder pedals that have had the pedal sides cut away and thinned to create a more accurate representation.

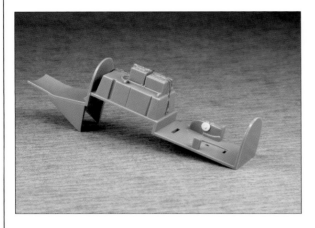

Here you see some minor details that were added to both the floorboard, rear left console and radio deck.

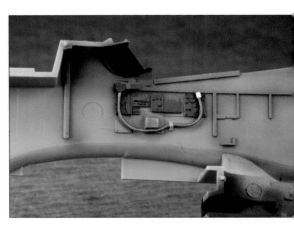

Some simple painting has been done to the starboard fuselage and you can see the oxygen hose detail now in place. Now all that is left is further painting.

The wearing away of the interior green paint reveals the wood fabrication of the floorboard.

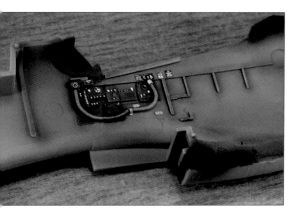

The completed and painted starboard cockpit wall. The Eduard P-51 placard set has been used to add a level of detail and interest that otherwise would be lacking.

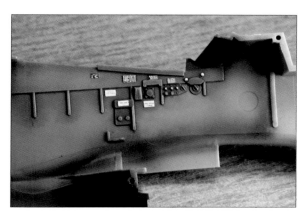

The port side of the cockpit has also been painted and detailed, again using the wonderful Eduard pre-painted placard set.

You can see that here a lot of depth has been created by pre-shading and then over-painting the cockpit with an interior green mix. As much detail as possible was pulled out using Vallejo acrylic paints.

The instrument dials have been punched out of an old AeroMaster P-51 decal sheet using a Waldron punch set.

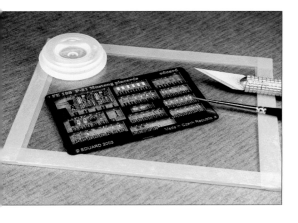

This is the Eduard Zoom set for P-51 placards. A simple X-Acto knife was used to cut them off of the fret and then a drop of Testors' Glosscote was used to attach them to the fuselage walls.

Here is the completed cockpit with all detail in place and painted.

remaining piece down to the actual size and mounted it to the sidewall. The only thing left was to touch up the floorboard paint. The cockpit was pre-shaded with dark grey, and then painted with a mix to represent interior green. All of the details were picked out with a brush using Vallejo Model Color acrylic paint and a fine brush. Although no instrument dial decals come in the kit, a set was punched out of an old AeroMaster decal set. Once the decals were in place and dry, a drop of clear fingernail polish was added over them to represent the glass. All that was left was to add some placards from the Eduard P-51 placard set, and then a pin wash of Payne's grey oil paint thinned with Turpenoid to the recessed areas. I drybrushed some highlights with a very small amount of titanium white oil paint.

General assembly

At this point, all of the cockpit elements were glued into the fuselage. The fuselage was then glued together and the wings glued in place. Virtually no gap was found at the wing roots but, just to play it safe, I ran a piece of Tamiya tape from wingtip to wingtip until it was dry.

The fuselage has now been glued together and the wings are mounted and in place. A strip of Tamiya tape has been used from wingtip to wingtip while the glue is setting to make sure there is no gap at the wing roots.

The aircraft that I am modelling does not have the fillet normally seen on P-51D Mustangs, so that area of the model has been ground away.

The resulting gap has been filled with scraps of Evergreen plastic and superglue. Although not aesthetically pleasing at this point, it ended up being sufficiently sturdy for the job.

All of the appropriate reshaping has been done. Here you can see not only the filling of the resulting gap, but the creation of the fairing plate that attached the upper rudder surface to the fuselage has been recreated using superglue and Tamiya putty.

Early in the process, I decided I was going to use the Ultracast replacement spinner. A great deal of modification has to be done to the nose to use it. Ultimately, if I were to do it again, I think I would use the kit spinner.

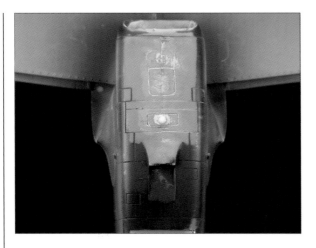

This shot shows the air intake on the lower fuselage with detail having been re scribed and replaced using scrap plastic.

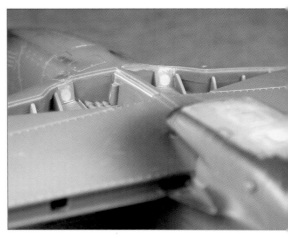

The wheel wells were not going to have a great deal of detail added to them, but I did want to remove the ejection-pin marks on the forward edge of the walls.

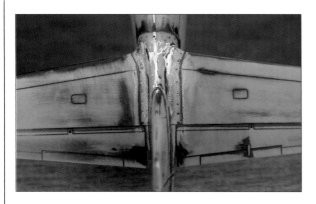

Once again you see the filled area where the fillet has been ground away, the metal fairing that attaches the vertical stabilizers to the fuselage, and the characteristic offset of the rudder that compensated for the rotation of the propeller.

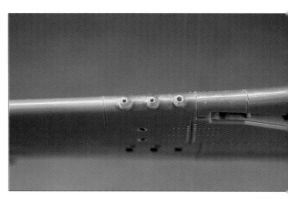

The kit gun barrels were very carefully cleaned up with an X-Acto knife and drilled out using a pin vice and drill bit.

I wanted to drop the flaps and Tamiya very graciously provides that option in this kit, but there is a recessed area in that flap that is provided in case you want to mount them in the up position. This had to be filled with plastic and the area further refined.

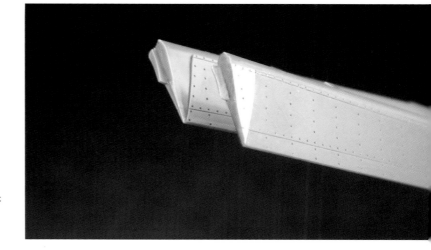

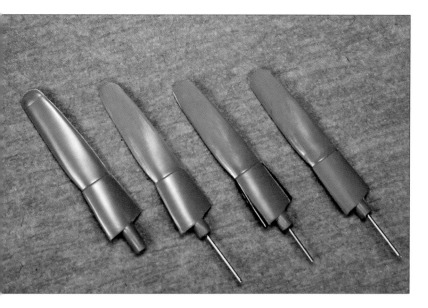

I decided to use the kit-provided propellers with some modifications. Each blade was sanded smooth, removing the bulbous tip at the end of each blade. As the kit's cuffs are too wide, each propeller blade was marked for the proper width cuff that was then ground away, smoothed, and ultimately pinned with brass rod to mount to the spinner.

Now it was time to turn my attention to removing the tail fillet. As 'Frenesi' was an early P-51D it flew without this particular feature. There are two ways you can fix this issue. You can purchase the very nice Ultracast conversion for just this issue or you can choose to do it the hard way. I chose the hard way! The first part was easy, using a Dremel tool and a medium grinding head to remove the moulded-in fillet. Once this was complete, I filled the resulting hole with scraps of plastic stock and glued it all in place with a generous amount of Zap-A-Gap. One spray of glue accelerant and I was ready to grind again, only this time I used a fine head and then took it down to its final shape using sanding sticks. With the easy part done, I then began to create the fairing that

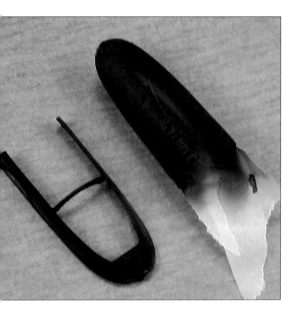

Probably one of the more awkward elements of this model was the way the clear canopy attached to the canopy frame. Both elements were pre-painted tyre black before the clear upper part was glued to the grey plastic lower frame.

Here you see the frame in the canopy glass glued and polished smooth.

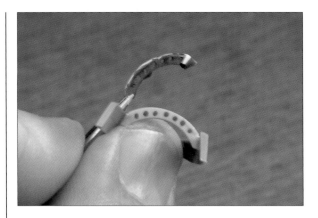

Although I was originally going to replace the canopy frame brace with the one provided by Ultracast, it is too narrow causing the frame to pinch in, so I ended up using it as a template for drilling the lightening holes that are characteristically in this brace.

As far as the external stores go for this model, I opted to use the Teknics paper drop tanks. I felt it was the best answer available when compared to the kit tanks, which are very hard to glue together while retaining all of the subtle detail.

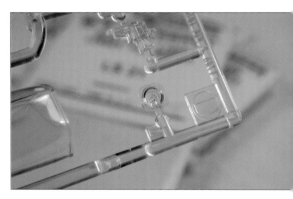

Here you see the completed paper drop tanks painted and cleaned up next to how they come in the Teknics set. A great deal of clean-up and filling has to be done to produce a quality presentation.

The landing light needed some additional detail, such as an MV lens for accuracy.

To accommodate the MV lens, I used a grinding tip to grind away the kit lens and create a pocket to glue the new lens into.

Here you see all detail added to the landing light. Not only has the new lens been put in place, but also the wooden wheel and its bracket created out of wire and Zap-A-Gap.

After taking a close look at the kit gunsight, I decided to use the Cutting Edge replacement with additional details in the way of wiring and the clear acetate reflector lens.

Some of the additional detailing and refinement that has been added to the landing-gear struts. Not only has it been plumbed, but also the openings in the scissors have been drilled out and opened up using an X-Acto blade.

blended the tail area into the rear part of the fuselage. This wasn't easy because t needed to be represented with a very thin, but refined, shape. Drops of slow-setting CA glue were added to the surface drop by drop in the approximate shape of the fillet and then sprayed with accelerator. I then went through the low process of refining the shape through sanding and using a blade to 'cut' a clean edge. A few times during the process I sprayed it with whatever paint I happened to have in the airbrush just to check where I was in the process. After all of the sanding, filling and testing was complete, a thin and precise shape was left. I added the rivet detail with a rivet punch and was done.

Now that the tail surgery was complete, I moved onto other details such as the spinner, which was replaced by the Ultracast offering. Small surface details and panel lines lost when gluing the fuselage together were added back at this point. The landing-gear bays aren't bad except for two large pushpin marks in the forward bay walls. With those filled, I decided not to add too much more and just see what I could do with them by just adding a good paint job. Again, it would be very easy to use tubing to represent the gun barrels but if you take your time, clean up and drill out the ones that the kit provides they can look fairly convincing. Although the kit gives you an option to mount the flaps in

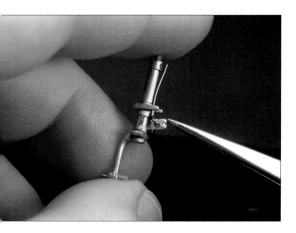

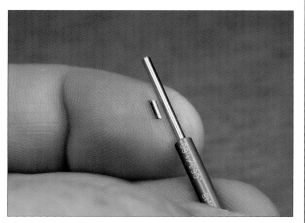

ere the landing-gear strut has been painted, and to create the ghly polished oleo, a small strip of bare metal foil was used and en attached using Testors' Glosscote.

From the Eduard Color placard set, the information plaque at the top of the struts was added by rolling the plaque itself on a fingertip using the Mission Models multi-tool.

the up or down position, Tamiya had to make a compromise so the flap, mounted in the 'up' position, would fit snugly to the outer wing faring. To do this, they created a recessed area for the upper wing fairing to rest in. If you want to display your flaps in the 'down' position, that recessed area needs to be filled with plastic. Once this was sanded and blended in, I simply added the rivet detail into the new plastic.

At this point, most of the surface detail was complete so I turned my attentions to the 'appendages' of the build. First came the propeller blades. At first, I had intended to use the cuffed blades included with the Ultracast spinner but I couldn't get all four of them to 'de-warp' to the same degree so I decided to refine the kit blades. These needed the tips sanding down and the cuff reduced to the correct shape. Once this was completed, I pinned them with brass rod so I could drill a hole in each blade socket in the resin spinner. I then used the brass rod to allow refining the angle and position of each blade without just sticking and committing with glue. Next the canopy. Because I used the latest release of this kit, I was fortunate enough to get the refined canopy created for this version. The attachment point from the sprue to the part is far less invasive and thus doesn't create an irreversible mark as in the older issues. The thing you do have to deal with is you need to glue a clear bubble to an opaque frame. In the real aircraft no attachment is visible in this area, so ideally it would be great to have the same effect on the model. The problem is, I don't think it can be done. I went through five canopy sets in an attempt to figure this one out. The best results came from spraying the edges that were to be glued together a light black colour and then using Tamiya ultra thin cement to glue the two pieces together. The bond was very good and, to a decent extent, the black paint hid the glue line. Once polished, I painted the frame but moved the demarcation line between the frame and the glass up a little to hide any other evidence of the glue line. The frame brace was going to be the Ultracast replacement part as it is much more of a scale thickness and has the lightening holes drilled in place, but the part is too narrow. When it is glued in place, the canopy glass is too wide. The solution is to thin down the kit brace and use the resin one as a template for the lightening holes. Spray through the Ultracast part and you have perfect marks to drill out the kit part. As for the 105-gal. compressed-paper drop tank, I gave up on the kit ones and went to the Teknics set. The landing gear light and its mounting bracket are moulded as one piece in clear plastic. When you pair

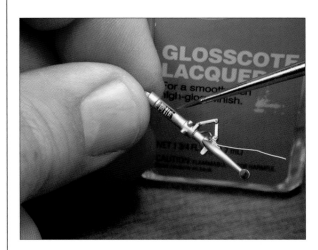

That plaque was then attached to the strut using a dab of Testors' Glosscote.

The finished and painted landing gear strut. The red element at the bottom of the strut is the tow hook, which was created by a simple piece of copper wire bent into a loop, CA glued to the end of that fork and painted red.

everything interior green, you can still see the moulded-in bracket through the lens face. I decided to grind it out and replace it with an MV lens as it gave it a more convincing look. The small wooden wheel that is attached using a bracket from the bottom of the light was added by making it out of copper wire and a few drops of Zap-A-Gap.

The reflector gunsight was from Cutting Edge; all it needed was a few wires and a clear acetate lens. The last thing to be created was the landing gear. The scissors were opened up to show the A-frame look, and then plastic fittings and copper wire plumbing were added. The towering at the end of the fork is just a circle of copper wire CA glued into place. They were painted aluminium using Alclad paints then a strip of Bare Metal Foil 'Polished Chrome' was used to highlight the oleos. Lastly, the strut plaque was bent to shape and attached with a drop of Testors' Glosscote.

Painting and markings

The entire plane's panel lines were painted with Gunze Tyre Black. I then painted all of the areas that need to either end up as white, or have a white undercoat, with a mix of Tamiya Flat White and a drop of Buff. Once that was

The aircraft is ready for paint. Pre-shading has been done to the undersurface and wheel wells.

Here you see the upper part of the aircraft with pre-shading on all panel lines and recessed areas.

First colours first. White was painted in broad strokes where we will eventually have invasion stripes and identification stripes. It was also used as an undercoat for the yellow spinner. Yellow is then over-sprayed.

Next step is to mask off the white areas of the invasion stripes preparing to spray the black stripes next. Here you also see the spinner has been masked and the red at the tip of the spinner has been sprayed.

done, I painted the chrome yellow base colour of the spinner. All that was left before I could paint the olive drab and neutral grey was to mask off the area to stay white. From this point forward it is pretty standard stuff: a clear coat of acrylic floor polish where the decals go and, once the decals are in place, another clear coat of floor polish and ultimately a light buffing with some 1,200-grit steel wool. Chipping was achieved by using a silver Prismacolor pencil and the panel lines were highlighted with Payne's grey oil paint thinned with Turpenoid.

Final touches

Last things last. All of those 'appendages' are now glued in place, including the drop tanks and their plumbing made of solder wire, the landing gear and doors, the pitot tube, etc. The model was sprayed with a final dusting of Testors Dullcote and the canopy was set in place with white glue.

This shows a mask that has been created to replicate the size and position of stars and bars on the side of the fuselage. Tamiya tape was used and this was done so that an even-coloured surface will be beneath an otherwise transparent white star.

After the olive drab and neutral grey paint was applied, all the decals were put in place and covered with acrylic floor wax. Once that was dried, the decal areas were lightly sanded using ultra-fine steel wool.

This shows the delicate process of adding the checkerboard stripe behind the spinner. Each individual red checker was cut from the AeroMaster decal sheet and applied one by one.

Here you see the upper surface after painting and decaling.

Again, the airplane has been painted and decaled. The lower surface has begun to be weathered using oil paint and MIG pigments.

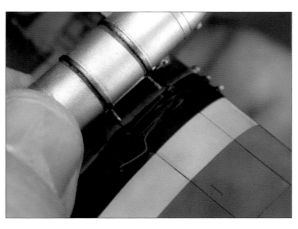

The plumbing for the drop tanks was added using solder wire. The aftermarket tanks are now pinned with copper wire and mounted to the wing rack.

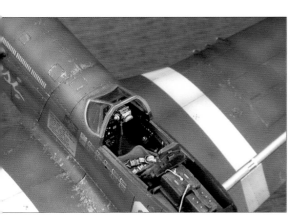

This shows the cockpit area without the rear canopy in place. Chipping has been created using a Prismacolor bright silver pencil.

In this shot, the chipping and weathering are shown to be effective at this scale. Care must be taken not to overdo the weathering as it can go too far very quickly.

The starboard side of the finished aircraft.

The port side of the finished aircraft.

This shot shows the degree of tonality put into each colour to attempt to tell a story with the final paint job.

Building a Korean War F-51D

Subject:	*F-51D*
Modeler:	*Brian Criner*
Skill Level:	*Intermediate*
Base kit:	*Tamiya*
Scale:	*1/48*
Additional detail sets used:	*Obscuro wheels; Ultracast flaps and rudder (48139 and 48008); Ultracast exhaust stacks (48009); Ultracast spinner and prop blades (48136); Aires wheel well (4219); Eduard Color photo-etch placards (FE198); Eduard seat harness, instrument panel and tailwheel doors (49268); Verlinden rockets (1407) and custom napalm tanks*
Decals:	*From kit*
Paint:	*Alclad on wings, Testors' Model Master Metalizer Aluminium Plate (Buffing) on fuselage, Testors' Model Master enamels*

Starting out ... the cockpit

I decided to forego the use of any aftermarket resin in the cockpit. Instead, I made use of the beautiful Eduard Color photo-etch sets. I recreated the seat supports, the oxygen regulator, the handle on the lower portside cockpit and various parts of the radio compartment using plasticard sheet and rod. Initially, I used a piece of stretched sprue to represent the oxygen hose on the starboard side of the cockpit but I later replaced this with a fine-gauge spring, cut to size.

When Mustangs were reactivated during the Korean War, many of them were still painted in the factory-applied interior green. Before they entered the conflict, all the cockpits were over painted with flat black. Since this was done quickly, the paint jobs were not of the best quality and, in most cases, the black paint quickly flaked off exposing the underlying interior green. To simulate this, I began by painting the cockpit with Testors' Interior Green enamel. I then applied a liberal coat of Future floor wax over the green to act as a protective barrier. When the Future was dry, I applied a couple of thin coats of Testors' Flat Black followed by some post-shading. I then added some Blue Magic plastic-polishing compound to a bottle cap and, using a toothpick with the point clipped off, I applied this to the areas of the cockpit that tended to get the most wear and tear, such as the cockpit floor, the seat tub and various parts of the sidewalls. I rubbed the compound in until I began to gently wear through the black, exposing the interior green underneath. In order to simulate the sharper, more pronounced scratches, I used a fine-point scribing tool and gently scraped away the surface paint.

After some modest dry brushing to pull out details, I added some Eduard Color photo-etch placards to the sidewalls and instrument panel, as well as Eduard's coloured seat belts. The throttle was replicated using a piece of cut syringe tubing. Once all of the pieces were in place, I went back and carefully added bits of chipping to the sidewalls using a Prismacolor chrome pencil sharpened to a fine point.

Fitting the Aires wheel wells

Mustang models sporting the amazingly detailed resin wheel well plug offered by Aires have always impressed me. I have also been intimidated by the prospect of

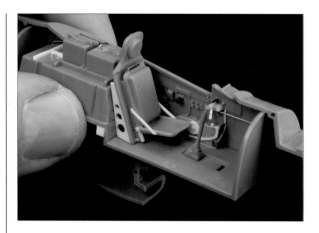

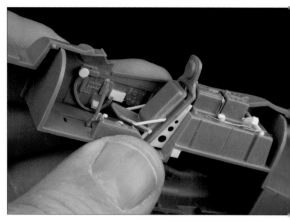

Rather than add a resin aftermarket set, the Tamiya cockpit was updated using pieces of plasticard rod and sheet plastic.

The oxygen hose was originally recreated using stretched sprue. Later, this was replaced with a very fine-gauge spring. Wiring in the radio compartment was replicated with fine copper wire.

The Tamiya seat is nice, but easily improved by adding styrene supports. The seat was finished out using coloured seat belts from Eduard.

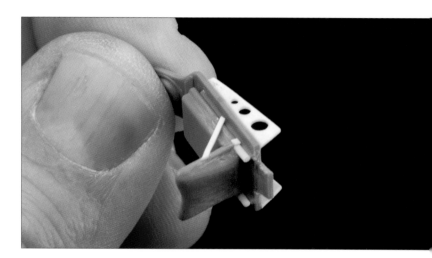

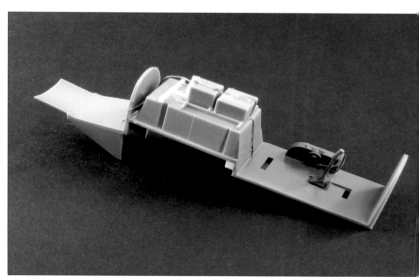

With modifications in place, the cockpit was painted with Testors' Interior Green enamel.

The interior green was given a protective coat of Future floor wax and then over painted in Testors' Flat Black. In order to show wear through the black to the underlying green, a toothpick, dipped in Blue Magic plastic polish, was used to gently rub through the surface paint.

The plastic polish creates a finely graded wear pattern through the surface paint. Scratches and blunt scuffs were recreated by gently picking at the surface colour with a pointed object. I used a scribing tool. A sewing needle would work just as well. Of course, it is important to pick at the paint gently to avoid scraping all the way to the grey plastic.

The addition of Eduard Color photo-etch placards and details to the cockpit sidewalls really brings the cockpit to life.

Weathering of the cockpit floor was carried out using a cotton bud dipped in Blue Magic plastic polish.

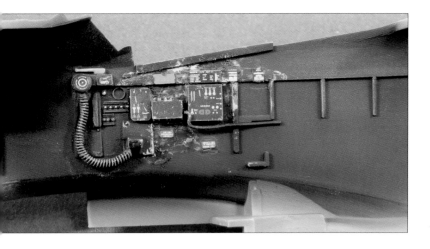

I had originally used stretched sprue to recreate the oxygen hose. I later decided to swap this out with a very fine-gauge spring. Inside the spring, painted black, is a piece of stretched sprue that was used to fasten the spring to the sidewall.

45

The top and bottom portions of the wing needed to be sanded and ground as thin as possible in the wheel well areas in preparation for the installation of the Aires wheel well plug.

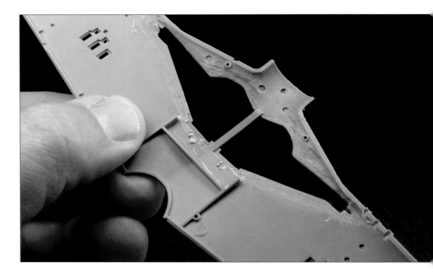

The wheel well was first painted black before receiving its topcoat of Testors' Chromate Yellow. Though the Aires resin wheel well insert is beautifully detailed, it is a challenge to get it to fit properly in the wing.

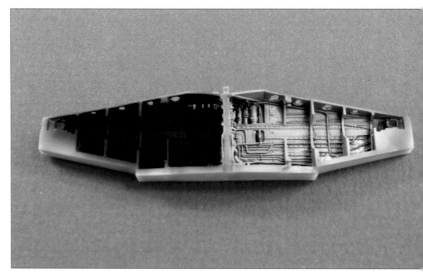

A testimony to the problems faced while trying to fit the Aires wheel well. The top and bottom wings were sanded eggshell thin. When cleaning up seams after the wings were together, the wing leading edge cracked in several places. Filling the openings with Zap-A-Gap glue and then sanding and polishing with various grades of sandpaper repaired the wing.

rying to get it to fit. Having used Aires resin wells on other projects, I knew there would be a lot of test-fitting and sanding before I was able to get that part to fit properly. I decided all of that beautiful detail would definitely be worth the effort. As there was going to be a natural metal finish on this aircraft, it was essential that the fit of this part be clean, as I wanted to avoid use of filler if at all possible. It took three attempts before I was able to thin the wing enough without destroying it. After assembling the fuselage halves, and gluing the top and bottom parts of the wings, I mated the wing to the fuselage. There was just one small gap in the leading edge of each wing, right at the wing/fuselage joint. and I applied a small dab of Zap glue, waited for it to dry enough to sand, and then began gently sanding the wing. While sanding that leading edge patch, the wing cracked due to the thinness of the plastic. Initially, I tried repeating the process, but this resulted in more cracking. Eventually, I took a toothpick and just hacked through most of it. Once I was satisfied that I had exposed all of the weak parts of the wing edge, I filled the entire space in the wing edge so that this issue would not crop up again. This whole process had also irretrievably damaged the wing gun stubs, so I drilled them out and added some tubing.

Time to paint

Since most natural metal finish (NMF) Mustangs had silver-painted wings, I wanted to vary the appearance of the silver on the wings compared to the fuselage. For the fuselage, I decided to use Testors' Model Master Metalizer Aluminium Plate (Buffing) and for the wings, Alclad's White Aluminium. I applied various shades of the Aluminium Plate to certain panels to show variation in the shade of silver typically seen in NMF aircraft. Before painting, I polished the entire aircraft with polishing cloths varying in coarseness from 3,600 to 12,000 grit. Next, I used a polishing wheel chucked in a Dremel tool to polish the surface to a glass-like shine. When I was satisfied that the surface was smooth and scratch free, I sprayed the entire surface with Mr Surfacer 1000 and then polished the surface with a Dremel tool again. Now I had a beautifully smooth, primed surface to spray the silver on. A smooth primed surface is especially important if you are using buffable Testors' Aluminium Plate, as the paint is fragile and easily rubbed off. After painting the fuselage and wings, I masked off a few panels around the aircraft and sprayed them with various shades of the paint to give the model some tonal variety. These panels were subsequently polished, along with the fuselage section, with a buffing wheel and then sealed with Future floor wax.

With the wing repaired and all seams and surface defects addressed, the model was painted. Alclad White Aluminium was used for the wings while Testors' Model Master Metalizer Aluminium Plate (Buffing) was used for the fuselage and tail. Notice that the anti-glare panel is incorrectly painted in this photo. The mistake was later corrected through careful masking and painting.

Future floor wax was applied to the entire model in preparation for decal application and weathering. All decals were stock, kit-derived decals.

Once all decals were on, they were sealed with Future floor wax. Next, the landing gear was installed and control surfaces and spinner attached. In preparation for the surface wash, the model was given a coat of Testors' Clear Flat.

Decals

Rather than search for an aftermarket set, I opted to use decals provided in the kit. All of the decals went down with few problems, though the shark's teeth did require some 'encouragement' in the form of numerous applications of Micro-Sol. After 95 per cent of the decals were on, I realized I had made a rather stupid mistake. I discovered I had improperly masked the anti-glare panel in front of the windscreen. The anti-glare panel is supposed to start at the bottom of the side windowsills and slope slightly upward to the nose. I had painted the panel parallel to the long axis of the aircraft straight to the nose and, because of that, I would be unable to apply the nose art lettering that was supposed to sit right above the port-side exhaust stacks. After some careful masking, I was able to correct the mistake and apply the nose art decal.

Weathering

Since this model represents a plane that was in a rugged, active duty environment, it was going to need to be more thoroughly weathered than an NMF Mustang in

These aircraft operated in harsh conditions and often flew several sorties per day. Dirt and grime from the feet of ground personnel left the wing walk areas full of grime and scuff marks. To replicate this, I applied MIG Productions' Vietnam Earth pigment with a chisel-tip brush to the wing walk areas. I then used an applicator to run some Tamiya liquid cement down the seam and through the pigments. A Prismacolor pencil was used to recreate metal scuff marks within the dirt-coloured stains.

The Tamiya flaps were swapped for the more accurate Ultracast flaps.

Weathering on the bottom of the aircraft was achieved by 'dusting' the wing with various shades of MIG pigments in the direction of wind flow across the wing. Oil and coolant leaks were simulated by applying blobs of burnt umber oil paint into various seams, then drawing them back with a flat-tipped brush slightly moistened with Turpenoid. The tyres and wheels were weathered by first running Tamiya liquid cement into the wheel/tyre seam and then dusting pigments into the cement using a fine-tip brush. This was then blended with a cotton bud.

The sliding canopy supplied by Tamiya comes in two parts, a lower frame and upper clear part. It is tricky to assemble these parts without damaging the clear part. The best technique for attaching the clear part to the frame is to line it up, then carefully run Tamiya liquid cement into the seam. Once the glue was dry, I lightly sanded the seam and then masked off the frame just above the seam line.

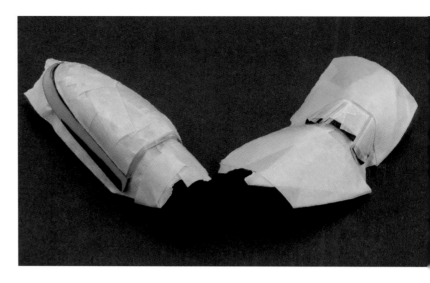

the European Theatre of World War II might have been. Normally, I don't spray anything over a metallic finish. This type of finish is delicate, even with th primer, so not adding a protective sealant is risky. In spite of this, a non-sealed metallic paint job, when properly polished, is a beautiful thing. If a sealer is used you are less likely to lose paint, but you will dull the beautiful sheen that you can only get with metallic paint, defeating the purpose of using it in the first place. In this instance, my goal was to vary the metallic effect, with some areas showing a dull surface, and other areas maintaining a sheen.

Since the wings were painted with Alclad, which is resistant to the effects of the wash, I added Grumbacher's oils liberally to all panel lines and recesses Once the paint had thickened a bit, it was wiped clear with cotton buds that had been dipped in Turpenoid, a turpentine substitute. Once the excess was removed, the wing area received another coat of Testor's Clear Flat to seal th wash. For the fuselage, painted with the very fragile metallizer, I first sealed th paint with a light coat of Future floor wax and then added a very conservativ wash, gently wiping out extra wash with a cotton bud. The key is to tak your time and use only gentle pressure (and very little Turpenoid) when wipin down the plane. To get my metallic sheen back, I followed this by carefull polishing certain areas of the aircraft with a buffing wheel.

Shrouded exhaust stacks from Ultracast were used in place of the Tamiya offering. They were weathered using the Rustall system.

Weathering on the anti-glare panel and canopy frame was accomplished with a sharpened Prismacolor chrome pencil. Arming wires were made from clear nylon thread.

used an Ultracast rudder and flaps in place of the kit items.

Once the wash was on, I turned my attention to other weathering effects to be applied. The exhaust stacks were 'rusted' using the Rustall products. Wing walk areas and various other parts of the aircraft were lightly brushed with MIG Productions' Vietnam Earth pigment. Since wing walk areas were likely to have extensive scuffing in addition to mud and dirt, I used a Berol Prismacolor chrome pencil to apply small chips to those areas. To replicate a heavily weathered anti-glare panel, I once again used my handy Prismacolor pencil. Exhaust staining and powder burns from the guns were recreated using a mix of Testors' Clear Flat, tinted with two to three drops of tan or buff, with a drop or two of flat black added. For a spray like this to be convincing the paint cup should be mostly clear, with just enough pigment to tint the solution. Your mix must be well thinned! If your mix is too thick, you will end up with a very fake-looking 'speckled' finish. As always, it is important to test spray on a piece of paper or post-it before applying to your model.

The prop and spinner are also Ultracast products. The resin prop blades need careful attention when inserting them into the spinner, as there are no guide tabs to ensure proper angle of attack. I used slow-drying Zap glue to attach the blade. Of interest, the stubs that are inserted into the spinner were painted. The Zap glue cured slower as a result, allowing me to adjust the blades after they were inserted in the spinner.

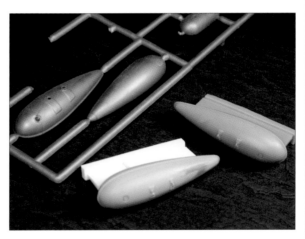

ABOVE François Verlinden specially cast the napalm tanks. This photo shows the difference between the resin tanks and those used to creat the masters from. Verlinden used a master created by Stan Spooner, which was a modified F-80 Shooting Star drop tank.

LEFT The aircraft is nearly complete. All that is left to be done is to add arming wires to the ordnance and complete the weathering of the anti-glare panel. The napalm tanks were painted with Testors' Chrome Yellow and were weathered with a wash of burnt umber oil paint after first receiving a coat of Clear Flat. The wash was then blown back across the structure using air from the airbrush.

The black painted area over the guns was peculiar to certain Mustangs in Korea. The strip runs along the bottom of the aircraft's wing onto the flap. Though I was not able to find any shots that showed this specifically, I am fairly certain this is the correct configuration for the top of the wing.

There is an arming structure of some sort on the napalm tanks that extends out of the filler cap. The arming wire loops down from the wing pylon and is attached to the top. I recreated this using a cut piece of syringe tubing.

Ordnance

Mustangs carried a variety of loads from 500lb bombs through 6in. HVAR rockets to napalm tanks. Many encounters were decided by the ability of Mustangs to put firepower on hard targets (such as tanks) at very short notice. This type of air combat was also extremely dangerous, with F-51s having one of the highest attrition rates of the war.

Though the Tamiya kit comes with all you need to give your Mustang a full load, I decided I would use Verlinden Productions' rockets instead of the kit items. I decided to use napalm tanks instead of bombs because I thought it would be fun recreating all of the corrosion and gunk that archival photos show covered those tanks. Unfortunately, the Tamiya kit does not provide proper 110-gal. drop tanks (those used for napalm drops). These drop tanks were slightly larger than the standard drop tanks used by Mustangs for carrying fuel. The 110-gal. tanks had a filler cap in the top, front centre of the tank compared to an offset filler cap in the 80-gal. tanks. The items used on the model were actually specially cast by François Verlinden and mastered by Stan Spooner, who used a modified F-80 Shooting Star tank as his starting point. The rockets from Verlinden are beautifully done and I highly recommend them for projects like this. The parts consist of a resin rocket tube and a separate, resin warhead. The fins and mounting braces are photo-etch. Upon close examination of wartime photos, it is clear these rockets were even dirtier than the aircraft that carried them. Usually, the rockets were stored in outdoor ammunition dumps, and were heavily weathered by the harsh Korean climate. Weathering of the ordnance followed the same basic pattern as the rest of the aircraft, with liberal washes of burnt umber artist oils on a flat surface. Once the ordnance was mounted, I added arming wire made from clear nylon thread.

The canopy and windscreen were polished out using a polishing wheel chucked in a Dremel tool. If done carefully, you will end up

with an incredible shine and no heat damage. The key is to use the stitched, laminated polishing disc, not the cotton-looking disc

The yellow chromate napalm tanks are a beautiful contrast to the natural metal finish of the aircraft.

In order to give the ordnance some contrast, each piece was post-shaded with a lightened shade of the base colour, or Clear Flat with a drop or two of beige or white.

LEFT Despite the coat of Future over the fuselage paint, buffing with a polishing wheel has brought back the sheen of the natural metal.

This view shows very nicely the effects of weathering with MIG pigments along the wing roots.

Double the trouble – the F-82G

Subject:	*F-82G Twin Mustang Night Fighter 'Mid Night Sinner'*
Modeller:	*Stan Spooner*
Skill level:	*Master*
Base kit:	*Modelcraft F-82G Twin Mustang Night Fighter (48022)*
Scale:	*1/48*
Additional details parts used from:	*Monogram P-61 Black Widow 1/48 scale; Tamiya P-51D 1/48 scale; Tamiya A-1J Skyraider 1/48 scale; Tamiya P-47D Thunderbolt 1/48 scale*
Additional detailing sets used:	*Eduard F-82 photo-etch update (48190); Eduard Color photo-etch placards (FE198); True Details P-51D Mustang seats (48453); Verlinden P-51 under-wing stores set (1407); Squadron Crystal Clear Canopy (9585); assorted clear lens by MV Products; Ultracast P-51 Mustang spinner and cuffed propeller update sets (48136)*
Decals:	*Kit supplied, Scale-Master Propeller Markings*
Paints:	*Gunze Mr Color Tyre Black, Alclad Bright Aluminium, Tamiya Gloss Aluminium and additional custom colour mixes*

A quick look at Modelcraft's 1/48-scale F-82G in the box

When I first purchased this kit I had high hopes for it, as this is the only 1/48-scale injection-moulded plastic kit of this aircraft. When I took a close look at the individual sprue trees and the level of detail, or lack thereof, as well

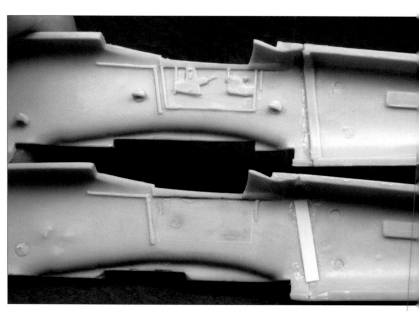

As you can see in the fuselage half at the top, the interior detail is severely lacking in the Modelcraft kit; what detail there was has been removed in preparation for the new interior.

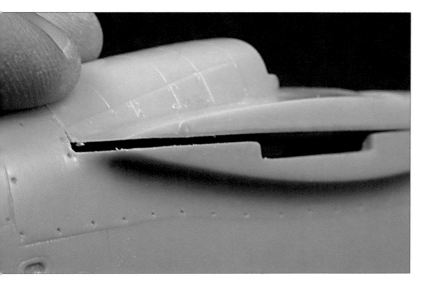

This is just one example of the fit issues that needed to be overcome. There was at least a 1/8in. gap between the lower-centre wing section and the left side of the pilot's fuselage.

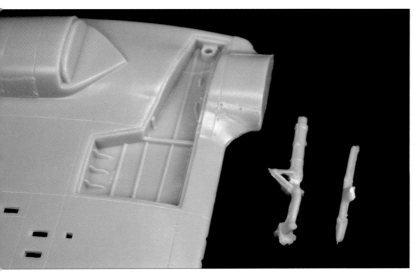

The main wheel wells are extremely shallow, lacking in any accurate detail. The main landing gear strut and retraction arms are grossly inaccurate and nondescript. All of this will need to be addressed by starting over.

s the surface imperfections I knew I was in for a long and arduous task. If ou take a close look at the outside surfaces of the parts, you will find some ey issues to be dealt with. First, it almost looked as if layers of plastic have een peeled away leaving blotches all over the surface. Secondly, when it omes to interior detail, it doesn't have any to speak of. Thirdly, the kit was roportionally incorrect in certain areas. Some things I was going to have to ve with, such as the cord of the wing and some profile issues, but there were everal elements that just couldn't go without repair.

Things that absolutely needed to be fixed

he first thing I did was to sand the entire fuselage down and prime it with ome Mr Surfacer 1000. This primer allowed me to see what was left once I took ıy initial wet/dry sandpaper pass at the outer surfaces. A fair amount of time ras spent rescribing the outside of this airplane. Any remaining panel line etails were filled with CA glue and rescribed using one of four rescribing tools: Tamiya tool, Tri-Tool scribing tools, scribing saws and Mission Models' new cribing tips.

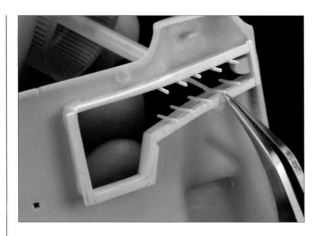

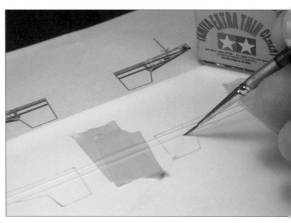

The wheel well reconstruction began by grinding out the old walls and roof and recreating them by using sheet plastic. Sidewall detail was added at this point using Evergreen strips, rod, wire and photo-etch panels from the spares box.

In order to understand the correct scale for the detail to be added to the wheel wells, I scanned the openings and saved them as a TIFF at 100 per cent size. I took that TIFF into Adobe Illustrator and designed detail to fit the opening. Once that was completed and printed out at 100 per cent, I had an exact template to refer to so I could accurately build the new detail.

The next task was to rebuild the landing gear bays. Since all of the operational photographs I could find of F-82Gs in theatre showed the larger inboard gear doors in the up position, I realized I needed to only detail the area where the open outer gear door revealed the landing gear bays. One of the things critically wrong on the kit is the depth of these bays: they are far to shallow. The entire upper surface of the gear bays was ground out using a Dremel tool. Once that was done I doubled the depth of the gear bays by facing the walls with .15in. plastic sheet. This is as deep as I could go without modifying the upper wing section. To come up with the detail I needed in the wheel well I used the photographs I had taken of the actual gear bays and drew them out using Adobe Illustrator. First I scanned the lower-centre wing section on my flatbed scanner with the roof of the wheel wells ground out. I saved the file as a Photoshop TIFF at 100 per cent and brought it into Adobe Illustrator. I traced the shape of the bay, and drew the hoses, wire

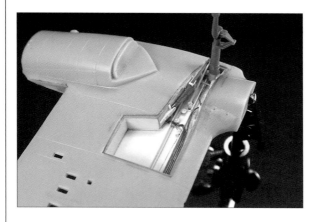

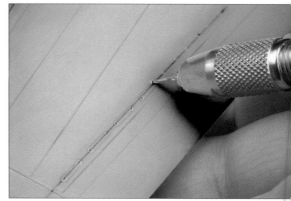

Here you see the completed wheel wells. There was not a lot of detail that needed to be added to the actual wheel bay as it was going to be covered by the main gear door. That door was almost always closed when the F-82 was on the ground.

The under-wing vents are represented in the kit as only some shallow engraved lines. On the actual aircraft, they are very large and open, so I felt that needed to be recreated. To do this, I started by drilling holes at an appropriate angle where these vent holes would exist.

Once enough holes were drilled, the holes were connected and opened up using an X-Acto knife blade and jeweller's files. You also see the opening that was created and boxed in with sheet plastic to accommodate the wing-mounted landing lights.

The ailerons were not cut out and actuated because I couldn't quite figure out how they would move! The F-82 had two sets of ailerons, inboard and outboard. I opted to just create the illusion of the forward edge of the ailerons being curved and going into the wing by laying Dymo tape along the wing and scribing that curve into the surface.

and other details in, essentially turning it into a template to build the new gear bays from. Sheet and rod plastic, different sizes and types of wire and an occasional piece of photo-etch from the spares box were used to create the bay details.

Next I drilled out the under-wing vents. When I look at the actual aircraft at the Air Force Museum, these vents are very pronounced and visible. In the kit some very shallow, elliptical panel lines represent them. I used my pin vice and .10mm drill bit and drilled through the centreline of those openings, making about four or five holes per vent hole at about a 30-degree angle. Once I had done that for each of the vent holes I used a No. 11 X-Acto blade and opened them up, connecting one to the next until I had a rough, elliptical opening at about a 30-degree angle. With jeweller's files and the No. 11 X-Acto blade, I was able to recreate a consistent set of vent holes more truly representing the

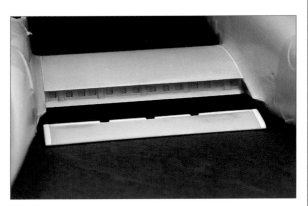

There was enough photo reference showing the flaps were often left in the down position so all of the flaps were cut out. By adding plastic stock, then grinding and sanding it to shape I got it to represent the correct profile. Here, you see the outer wing flap has had its shape modified. Also the wing itself has been filed and thinned to accommodate the new flap forward edge.

The centre wing flap has been cut out, modified, extended and detailed. The inner bulkhead was recreated using Evergreen sheet plastic. Where the flap should sit under the wing root, a recess had to be created by shaving back the lower section of the fuselage and thinning out the upper section. Once this was created, it was all boxed in with .10in. plastic sheet.

The horizontal stabilizer was modified by cutting the flap away and cutting free the tabs; they were then reshaped to be more accurate when shown articulated.

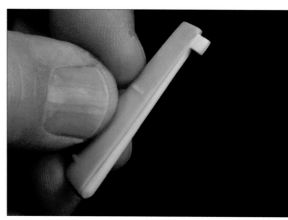

The rudders were cut free from the vertical stabilizers and then modified to have a correct shape. The vertical stabilizers were thinned to accommodate the new rudders. The actuators for the rudder tabs were cannibalized from Tamiya P-51 parts out of the spares box.

under-wing look. At this point I also created an opening under each wing for the missing landing lights to come out of. They were boxed in with sheet plastic and made ready for detailing at a later point.

The next large task to undertake was the actuating of the flaps and rudders. I cut them away from the kit wings and then created the airfoils by adding stock plastic to the leading edges prior to reshaping them. All of the main wing flaps need to be extended in width because on the real aircraft they nested up into a recessed area under the fuselage fillet. This recessed area was created by carefully cutting away the lower and upper fuselage to accommodate new wider flaps. Care had to be taken to leave a convincingly thin fillet. I extended the radiator air intakes forward to the correct length by again adding stock plastic to the appropriate areas and then sanding and filing it to shape. I joined some fine nylon screen to a piece of Evergreen sheet plastic using Tamiya super thin cement to create new radiator screens. These were then trimmed to shape and glued over the nondescript moulded-in kit screens.

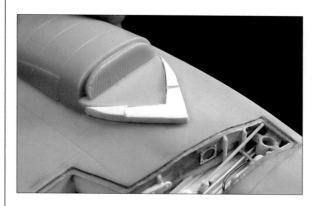

One of the structural shape flaws that can be addressed fairly easily is the depth of the intake splinter. Layers of plastic stock were cut to shape so I could extend the splinter to the correct depth and then superglued into place. The new leading edge of the intake splinters were then sanded and filled to fit.

The intake screens were recreated to better effect by using Tamiya extra thin cement to glue nylon screen to .10in. sheet plastic cut to shape.

Detailing, correcting, etc.

One of the largest issues for me on this kit was the radar pod. It is grossly misshapen in that it is provided completely round while clearly the radar pod had an elliptical cross section. So, I took the two halves of the pod and quartered it using a razor saw and shimmed those quarters out with some Evergreen strip to match the scale profile drawings from the Squadron book *P-51 in Action* blown up to 1/48 scale. I then ground, sanded and otherwise coaxed the pod into a fairly convincing cross section. I knew I wanted to try to detail the radar within the pod itself and to do this I needed to have the nose-cone radar pod separate so the radar dish would be exposed. I drew on the pod where I felt the nose cone would be, following line drawings and other reference, and cut it loose with a razor saw. Once that was all cleaned up, I glued in place the bulkhead that the new scratch-built radar would be mounted onto.

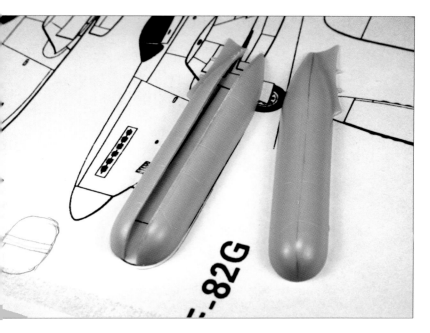

One of the other shape issues that absolutely needed to be fixed was the radar pod. The pod as provided has a circular cross section where the actual pod had an oval cross section. To change this, the two halves need to be cut down the centreline.

.125in. Evergreen plastic strip was then superglued into place. Once filed and sanded to shape, this will give the pod the correct profile.

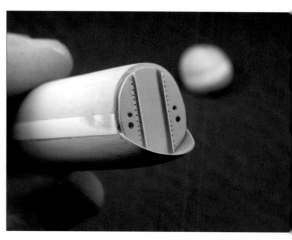

So the scratch-built radar can have a place to live, the end was cut off the pod using a razor saw.

A bulkhead was scratch-built using sheet plastic and plastic strip. Here you see it after being primed.

The information I have used to create that radar and associated bulkhead area is, at best, sketchy. There is a cutaway line drawing from an old issue of *Air Enthusiast* which showed the SCR 720C and some sort of amorphous mounting device and boxes in position. Using this, and the fact that the same radar was used in the P-61 Black Widow, I took the dish from a Monogram Black Widow kit and scratch-built the rest of the elements around it. The drawing didn't show any wiring or cabling, so I just added a few elements to create a bit of interest both out of copper wire, as well as heated and annealed piano wire to create a corrugated cable look. I created the actual tip of the radar cone by cutting a thin strip from a photo-etch frame and using the Mission Models multi-tool to wrap a perfect circle around. Once that was done, a small piece of Evergreen rod was added to the centre of the loop and this completed the radar.

Other areas that were recreated from scratch were the tail assembly and tailwheel bays, the hot air exhaust ramps and radiators and carburettor scoops. I also added Eduard photo-etch parts to better represent the air filter inspection panels and the fuel tank caps.

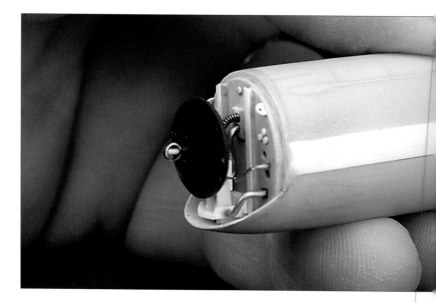

This was my best guess concerning the SCR 720C radar used in the F-82G. Everything was scratch-built except the dish, which was taken from a Monogram P-61 kit. The P-61 and the F-82 used the same radar system.

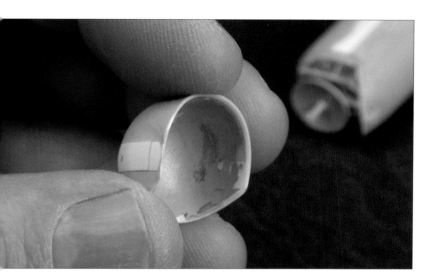

Here you can see the inside of the cone once it was thinned and smoothed out using a ball-shaped grinding tip on a Dremel tool.

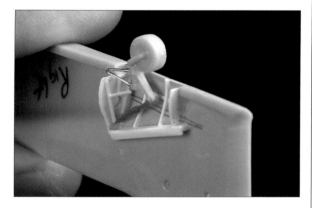

Both of the kit tailwheels were rebuilt using brass wire and strip plastic for the control mechanism. The retraction arms were taken from the spares box.

The tailwheel bays were created using Evergreen sheet and strips. The bulkheads and sidewall detail was once again a 'best guess' on my part. The rudder control wires were added using ultra thin copper wire.

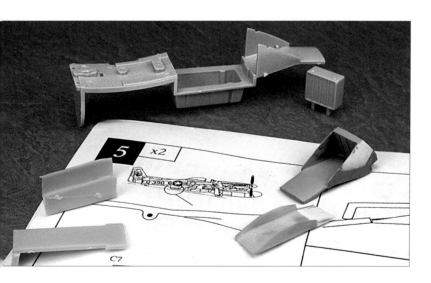

The parts provided in the kit for the hot air exhausts are extremely poor. On the left, you can see the kit parts. On the right, you can see the parts created to represent the radiators using parts cannibalized from some spare Tamiya P-51D parts.

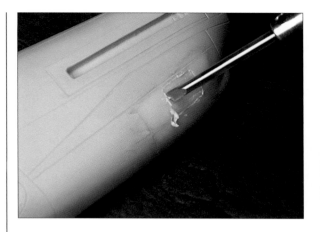

Since all the surface detail had to be redone, I used the photo-etched air filter inspection panel from the Eduard detail set to add a degree of refinement. I used the chisel set from Mission Models to remove the old detail and create a recessed area to set the new photo-etched panel into.

The carburettor intakes are badly misshapen. I solved this by opening up the area with a No. 11 X-Acto blade and then forming a .10in. plastic strip into the opening. Once this was glued into place, it was faired in using Tamiya basic putty.

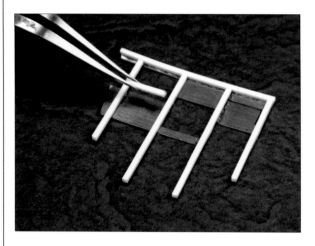

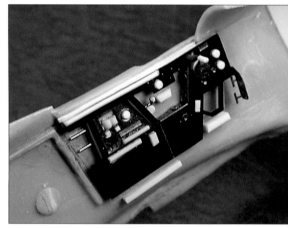

Some depth was added to the back of the Eduard cockpit sidewall sections by gluing some .15in. x .15in. strip using Zap-A-Gap.

Once the sidewall sections have been glued in place, the rest of the photo-etch parts and Evergreen bits have been added to create the right level of detail.

I really wanted the cockpits to be a showcase for detail, though there is not a lot of good documentation on the interior of this aircraft. Squadron did wonderful job of illustrating those cockpit walls in their Fighting Color series *P-5 Mustang in Color* and, with these illustrations in hand, the Eduard photo-etch detail set for the kit and additional references provided to me by the National Air Force Museum in Dayton, Ohio, I knew that there was a great deal of work to be done to improve both cockpits. First, I created some depth by adding plastic strip to the back of the Eduard cockpit sidewall. Once the sidewalls were glued in place, the rest of the photo-etch parts and Evergreen pieces were added to create the right level of detail. The radar operator's cockpit was detailed with not only photo-etched parts, but also plastic bits and copper wire. The photo-etched instrument panels added a nice touch with their level of detail and acetate dials, but some extra work was still needed. The pilot's instruments were sufficient but the radar operator had two appliqué panels that were improved by adding some

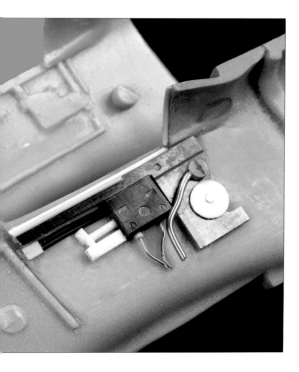

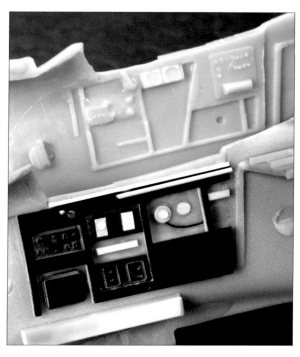

adar operator's port sidewall detail has been added with not nly photo-etched parts, but also plastic bits and copper wire.

The radar operator's starboard sidewall and deck detail behind the seat.

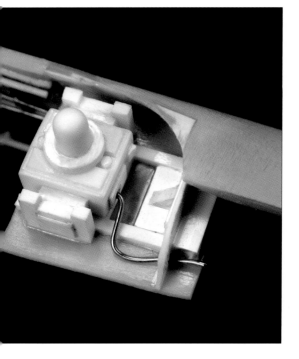

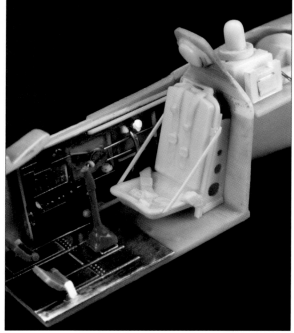

his shot shows the scratch-built loop antenna assembly behind e pilot's seat. There was not a great deal of detail available on is area so it was mostly based on a vague drawing found in a taway in an old *Air Enthusiast* magazine.

The pilot's cockpit before paint. This shot shows the rudder pedals and stick that have been taken and modified from a Tamiya P-51D kit. The seat and headrest were taken and modified from the True Details P-51 update set.

The radar operator's cockpit with scratch-built details on the sidewalls and the seat before paint.

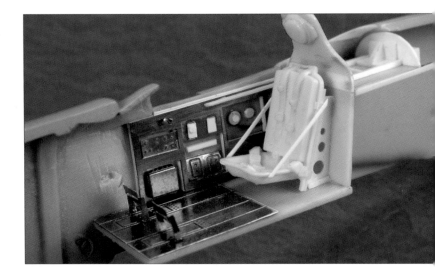

After paint, the radar operator's cockpit comes to life. Details have been picked out with Vallejo acrylics and a small brush.

The pilot's cockpit is airbrushed with a mix of Gunze Tyre Black and then highlighted with the same paint lightened with Tamiya Buff. Once again, the details have been picked out with Vallejo acrylics.

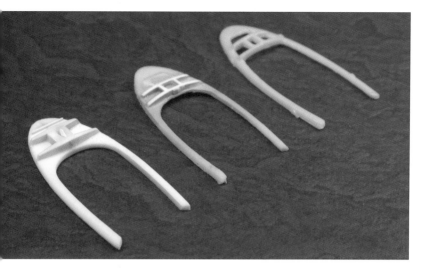

Here you can see the evolution of the canopy frames. On the right you can see the frame as provided in the kit. The centre shows the frame modified in an attempt to make it look more like the real thing. On the left is the scratch-built frame that was ultimately made to best represent the actual frame. The only work done to the frame after this shot was taken was the bottom centre area was thinned down to sit better on the back of the fuselage.

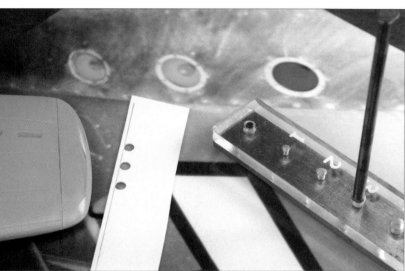

The under-wing formation lights are completely missing. In the background of this photo you see the actual lights as found on the F-82 at the National Air Force Museum. Sitting on top of the photo is the wingtip to be fixed and the plastic sheet with punched holes to represent those lights.

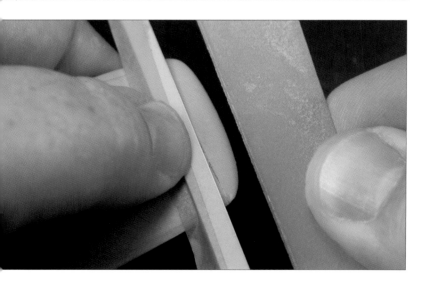

The wingtip was sanded down using a guide that has been taped to the wing along the panel line and a medium-grit sanding stick.

Once the lower surface of the wingtip was sanded down to match the depth of the .15in. plastic sheet, holes were punched through the plastic sheet to represent lights, then it was glued into place and sanded to shape.

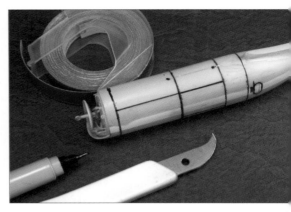

This shot shows the new panel lines needing to be scribed into the radar pod. Almost all panel lines on the kit were filled and then rescribed.

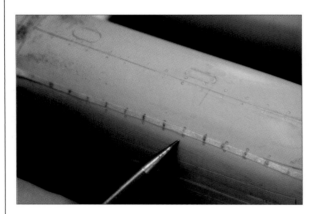

This is how I represented the Dzus fasteners on the engine cowling. A simple tape strip with hash marks at a consistent interval was set along the area to be marked and then I used the MDC punch tool to make the marks. It took a while, but the end result was worth it.

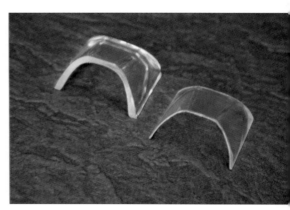

The clear parts provided are so thick that at scale they look like they would belong on a tank, not an aircraft. The Squadron vacuform replacement canopies were used instead.

Because the new windscreen was so much thinner, the contact points on the fuselage needed to be shimmed out using plastic strip.

sheet plastic to the backs for depth. The two radar screen vision covers were not included in the photo-etch set so I just cut a strip from the etch brass frame about ⅛in. wide by ¼in. long and then bent it into the appropriate oval shapes. The rim of the covers that needed to conform to the operator's face were ground to shape using a fine grinding wheel and the padded edge was created by painting (or dabbing) four to five layers of leather brown acrylic paint on the edge. The decks behind each seat needed to be built from scratch as no detail was provided in the kit. A scratch-built loop antenna assembly also needed to be mounted behind the pilot's seat. There was not a great deal of detail available on this area so it was mostly based on a very vague drawing found in a cut-away in old *Air Enthusiast* magazine. The rudder pedals and stick were taken and modified from spare Tamiya P-51D kits. The seats and headrests were taken and modified from the True Details P-51 seat set. After the paint was applied, the cockpits come to life. Details were picked out with Vallejo acrylics and a small brush. The cockpits were airbrushed with a mix of Gunze Tyre Black and then highlighted with the same paint lightened with Tamiya Buff.

Other details added or recreated were the canopy frames, under-wing formation landing lights and landing gear, brake systems and tyres. The gear struts were a 'Frankenstein' creation using the upper part of a set of Tamiya P-47 struts, the scissors and oleos from some spare P-51 struts, and a lower strut created from stock plastic carved to shape and lined with brass sheet for reinforcement. The rims and tyres provided in the kit are substantially undersized so they were replaced with the ones that come with Tamiya's Skyraider. The fourth brake pad 'puck' was made out of plastic stock and all of the plumbing and fittings were made from copper wire and fine solder.

The gunsight is a modified resin F-80 part from the Black Box cockpit set.

The 'Frankenstein' landing gear. The upper section of the strut is from a Tamiya P-47, the oleo and scissors are from a Tamiya P-51 and the lower section of the struts cut and shaped from plastic stock. Once the final shape was completed, a piece of .15in. brass sheet stock was cut and glued to the inside of the arm for added strength.

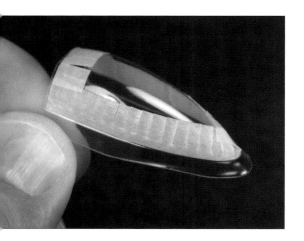

This is the Squadron canopy masked using Tamiya tape.

The rocket rail rack pylons were modified from P-47 parts. On the left, you see the original parts before being cut down and reshaped.

This is how the 'I'-shaped rocket rail frames were made. On the left are three sections of Evergreen stock glued together. In the centre is the plastic roughly cut to shape and on the right you can see the final air foil shape that was created by carving and sanding everything away that didn't belong.

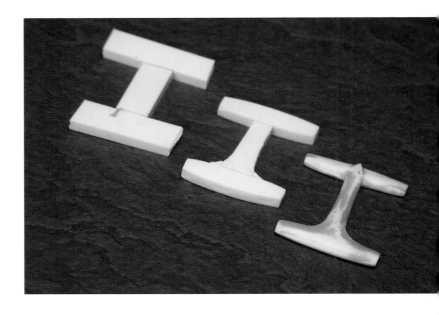

Each rocket rail frame has five attachment points, three 'up' and two 'down'. The Verlinden P-51 under-wing stores set was modified and used for these attachment points. The points in the second and fourth position were glued to a piece of plastic stock that was sanded to the shape of the attachment point and then glued in between the other three stations so that they would extend further away from the bottom of the frame.

Once the fuselages were closed up and wings were put together, I just needed to add a few last details. The gunsight was a modified resin piece taken from the Black Box F-80 cockpit set. I added an acetate reflector and some wiring. I also replaced the kit windscreens and canopies with the nice vacuform replacements by Squadron. Because the new windscreen was so much thinner, the contact points on the fuselage needed to be shimmed out using plastic strip.

The last thing to be created was the under-wing stores. The drop tanks provided are the wrong size and shape so I borrowed a set from my Monogram P-61 set and modified the pylons that came in the kit. I added an etched filler cap to the tanks. The rockets were going to come from the Verlinden under-wing stores set. Gluing the basic shape together out of strips of Evergreen stock and then grinding, filing and sanding them into the appropriate airfoil shape created the 'I'-shaped mounting rails. The rocket attachment points were modified from the Verlinden set. Once that was completed I created the pylon by modifying a pair of Tamiya P-47 pieces.

Ready for paint

The outer surface was now prepared for paint by giving the entire plane a coat of Mr Surfacer 1000. Once that was dry, it was time to give a light sanding with 1,200-grit wet/dry sandpaper to knock down any unseen irregularities. The entire airframe and all other elements were then sprayed with Tamiya's Gloss Aluminium from the can. It covered well and had a great finish. The entire aircraft was then covered with a few coats of Future acrylic floor wax as a barrier between the outer paint and the undercoat of silver when the chipping begins. Although F-82Gs in Korea were entirely black, I used a lot of other colours mixed with Gunze Tyre Black to represent fading, dirt, grime, etc. The wing roots were highlighted with mists of tans, greys and browns to represent the build-up of dirt. It is clear from the photos of F-82s in Korea that the black paint chipped fairly easily revealing the aluminium below so after painting all of the 'black' tones, a scalpel-shaped blade was used to 'chip' away the upper layer of paint. The chipping was most apparent at the wing roots, the leading edges of the wings and around the Dzus fasteners on the engine cowlings. A subtle transparent coat of 'dirt' was sprayed over the chips to cut the contrast

Now that the entire model is ready for paint, it has an overall coat of gloss aluminium with a heavy coat of acrylic floor wax. This creates a barrier when a blade is taken to the topcoat of black to simulate the chipping that was common on F-82s.

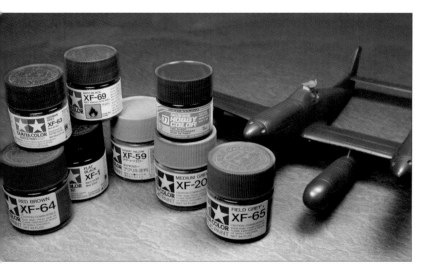

Although the aircraft were entirely black, I used a lot of other colours mixed with Gunze Tyre Black to represent fading, dirt, grime, etc.

After painting, a scalpel-shaped blade was used to chip away the upper layer of black paint.

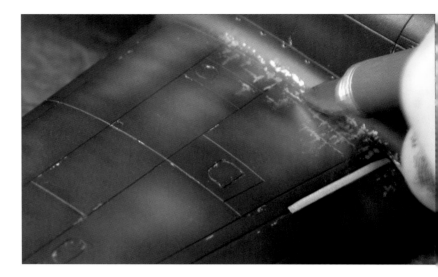

Most of the chipping has now been completed.

Here you see the chipping has a subtle transparent coat of 'dirt' sprayed over it to try to make the contrast between the chipped aluminium and the paint more to scale.

This is the finished landing gear and disc brakes. The tyres and rims are taken from a Tamiya Skyraider kit. These are substantially larger than the kit ones, but are correct for the aircraft. The only thing that needed to be added to the assembly was the fourth brake puck and all of the appropriate plumbing and fittings.

Here you see the starboard landing gear in mounted position. The landing light was modified from a Tamiya P-51 kit and added to this strut. An MV lenses was added for realism.

The scratch-built wing-mounted landing lights consist of a ¼ in. square hole cut in the appropriate outboard position on each wing. The doors and mounting brackets were made of sheet plastic. Lastly, I added MV lenses with the backs painted interior green. These lights show up in many photos but are not provided or even indicated on the kit.

The flame dampeners on the exhausts were modified using a razor saw to deepen the area between the blades. Coarse wet/dry sandpaper was folded over and run through the new cuts to open them up and thin out the blades. Finally, vertical support straps were glued at the leading edge of each set of three blades.

back a bit. It helped the chipping seem more appropriate for the scale. Th[e] decals were provided in the kit and went down just fine. They were set dow[n] on a coat of Future and then set with Micro-Sol. Once they were dry, an uppe[r] coat of Future was sprayed around the edges. When the Future was dry, it wa[s] smoothed out with extra fine steel wool and then the entire outside of th[e] model was sprayed with Testors' Dullcote. Although F-82s were delivered to th[e] front in gloss black, the finish quickly became dull with time in the dirt[y] forward operating bases. A few oil washes to the panel lines with Payne's gre[y] and burnt umber and some dusting of the landing gear with some MI[G] pigments and the paint was done. The last thing to be painted was the rada[r] cone. I found a great shot of 'Mid Night Sinner' flying with an unpainte[d] brown replacement cone, so I painted my model the same way.

The AeroProducts prop blades were going to be a problem. I looked through a lot of kits to see what I could use and the only thing remotely close was the blades that came with the Classic Airframes P-51H kit. They were reshaped, pinned with a brass rod and set into holes drilled into the Ultracast spinners.

Finishing touches and final thoughts

Now that the paint was done, all of the fragile elements needing to be added on to the plane were glued in place. The AeroProduct prop blades were modified from two Classic Airframe P-51H kits, as they were the only ones that were close enough to the final blade shape that I needed. The AeroProduct logos are from Lloyd Jones. The flame-dampening exhausts were modified from the kit part by using a razor saw and coarse wet/dry sandpaper to open up the distance between the blades of the exhausts. A vertical brace was added at the leading edge of each set of three blades with .10in. plastic strip. The starboard landing-gear light was detailed with an MV lens as were the scratch-built gun camera lenses, under-wing landing lights and rudder formation lights. The wingtip lights on the G model seemed to be teardrop in shape, so I used the Cutting Edge coloured clear light set to get two small lenses and glued them to the wing tips.

Here you see all of the custom-made elements built to go under the wings.

ABOVE A close-up of the 5in. HVAR rockets taken from the Verlinden P-51 stores kit; the arming wires are made from fishing line.

BELOW This shot shows the squat look and dropped flaps on the aircraft.

This is the articulated rudder with MV taillights lenses in place.

ELOW The overall look of the plane is dirty and war weary. Although the actual planes were
elivered in gloss black, the colour scheme rapidly became dull in the hostile environment.

ABOVE In this shot you can see all of the dropped flaps, chipped paint and weathering in all its glory. You can also see the 'unpainted' fibreglass radar cone in its cradle.

BELOW This was one big, low, wide and beautifully ugly aircraft.

ABOVE This shot gives a realistic impression of the width of the aircraft.

BELOW The radar housing was the F-82G's most distinctive feature.

Further reading and research

When it comes to finding out information about a subject as popular as the P-51, it isn't hard to go into a bookstore or complete a web search and find something useful. There are a lot of resources out there if you want to model one of the mainstream Mustangs such as the P-51A, B and the D. If you want to build one of the more unique versions such as the P-51H or the F-82 Twin Mustang that's a different matter. I filled in any information gaps by going over some old aviation publications that I have collected over the years such as *Air Enthusiast*. This magazine is valuable because it often provides great period photos and if you are lucky, a handy cut-away drawing of your subject. Another possibility is to look at the real thing! Because of the long-lasting love affair with this aircraft and because it hung around and was used for many years after World War II, it isn't hard to find P-51Ds to visit in museums throughout the US and worldwide though it may be a little harder to come across P-51As and Bs. As for the Twin Mustang, I arranged to visit the United States Air Force Museum in Dayton, Ohio, USA. One of the few remaining F-82s in the world reside there and the kind people at the museum were very helpful in providing me with information as well as allowing me to take photographs of this rare bird.

Further reading

Cabos, R. H., Osprey Modelling Manuals 19: *North American P-51 Mustang* Oxford: Osprey Publishing, 2002

Davis, L., *F-82 Twin Mustang Mini in Action 8* Carrollton, TX: Squadron/Signal Publications, Inc., 1996

Davis, L., *P-51 Mustang in Action* Carrollton, TX: Squadron/Signal Publications, 1981

Davis, L., *P-51D Walk Around* Carrollton, TX: Squadron/Signal Publications Inc., 1996

Davis, L., *Fighting Colors P-51 Mustang in Color* Carrollton, TX: Squadron/Signal Publications Inc., 1982

Ethell, J., *Warbirds: American Legends of World War II* Ann Arbor, MI: Lowe & B. Hould Publishers, 2003

Freeman, R., *Combat Profile: Mustang* London: Ian Allan Ltd., 1989

Freeman, R., *The Mighty Eighth in Color* Stillwater, MN: Specialty Press Inc., 1992

Green, W., and Swanborough, G., 'F-82: Killers Over Korea', *Air Enthusiast* 6, 1978

Green, W., and Swanborough, G., 'Mustangs in Korea', *Air Enthusiast* 15, 1981

Karnas, D., *P-51D Mustang*, Modelmania Three Gdansk: AJ-Press, 2005

Kinzey, B., *P-51 Mustang Part 1*, Detail & Scale Vol. 50 Carrollton, TX: Squadron/Signal Publications, 1996

Kinzey, B., *P-51 Mustang Part 2*, Detail & Scale Vol. 51 Carrollton, TX: Squadron/Signal Publications, 1997

Ludwig, P., *P-51 Mustang, Development of the Long-Range Escort Fighter* Surrey: Classic Publications, 2003

McLaren, D., *Double Menace P/F-82 Twin Mustang* Colorado Springs, CO: ViP Publishers, Inc., 1994

Nicholls, J., and Thompson, W., *Korea The Air War 1950–1953* London: Osprey Publishing Limited, 1991

Olmsted, M., *The 357th Over Europe* St Paul, MN: Phalanx Publishing Co., Ltd., 1994

Pape, G., Campbell, J., and Campbell, D., *Northrop P-61 Black Widow* Osceola, WI: Motorbooks International, 1991

Phillips, G., *Allison Engined Mustangs Walk Around No. 13* Carrollton, TX: Squadron/Signal Publications Inc., 1998

Shiwaku, M., Aero Detail 13: *North American P-51D Mustang* Tokyo: Dai Nippon Kaiga Co., Ltd., 1995

Shores, C., and Thomas, C., *2nd Tactical Air Force* Volume One Surrey: Classic Publications, 2004

Thompson, W., *Korea The Air War (2)* Oxford: Osprey Publishing Limited, 1992

Thompson, W., 'Double Trouble The F-82 Twin Mustang in Korea!', *Wings Magazine*, Vol. 13, No. 4, 1983

Verlinden, F., *Modeling, Detailing, Painting, Weathering WWII Aircraft* O'Fallon, MO: Verlinden Publications/The VLS Corp, 1998

Zurek, J., and Wisniewski, P., *North American P-51 Mustang P-82 Twin Mustang No. 57* Gdansk: AJ-Press, 2003

Websites

HyperScale http://www.hyperscale.com

Modeling Madness http://www.modelingmadness.com

Aircraft Resource Center http://www.aircraftresourcecenter.com

Index

References to illustrations are shown in **bold**.

80

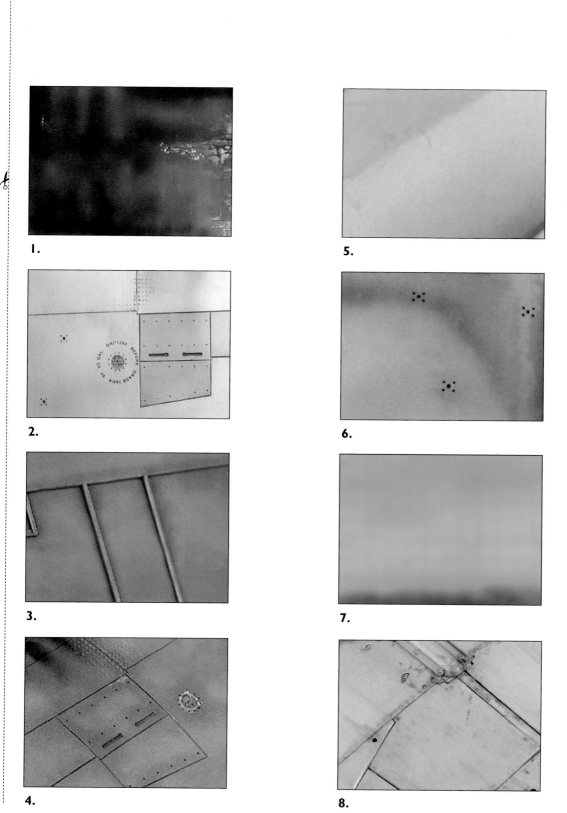

1.

5.

2.

6.

3.

7.

4.

8.

5. Chrome Yellow

The napalm tanks, spinner and wingtips of the F-51 were painted a heavily weathered chrome yellow based on photos from Osprey's *F-51 Units in Korea*. The photos of these tanks reflect extreme weathering from exposure to the elements and sloppy filling of the napalm into the tanks.

6. British camouflage colours

The upper-surface camouflage was painted RAF Dark Green and Ocean Grey. The lower camouflage was painted with RAF Medium Sea Grey. These were common colors within the RAF during this period.

7. ID Red

This colour was primarily used as a unit identifier and was represented by Testor's Model Master Enamels Italian Red. I chose Italian Red over Insignia Red because the former colour has a warmer tint to it.

8. Neutral Grey

This was the standard colour for the lower surfaces of USAAF aircraft during World War II. This area on an aircraft was not only exposed to the elements but also oil and grime from the engines and exhaust.

1. Night Fighter Black

Although the F-82 Twin Mustang was delivered entirely in gloss black, with the harsh environment and wear and tear, patches of dark grey-brown over a dull black is more representative of the actual colour of the aircraft.

2. Natural Metal

The fuselages on all of the F-51s that the USAF flew in Korea were bare aluminium. These aircraft sported laminar flow wings that were metal, with filled in seams, primed with chrome yellow and painted silver. All of these surfaces were heavily exposed to the elements

3. Interior Green

This is one of those colors that that is difficult to pin down precisely. Suffice it to say that it was a yellow-green colour that was applied to USAAF aircraft with few exceptions.

4. Olive Drab

This was one of the most prevalent exterior colors seen on USAAF P-51s early in the war. This upper-surface camouflage color was intended to blend into the landscape.